7MINUTES WITH JESUS

DAILY DEVOTIONS FOR A DEEPER RELATIONSHIP

FEATURING THE MESSSAGE® //REMIX™

TH1NK
P.O. Box 35001
Colorado Springs, Colorado 80935

TH1NK is an imprint of NavPress.
TH1NK and the TH1NK logo are registered trademarks of NavPress. Absence of ®
in connection with marks of NavPress or other parties does not indicate an absence of
registration of those marks.

ISBN 1-57683-814-5

Cover design by Mattson Creative
Cover photo by Hisham Ibrahim, Getty Images
Creative Team: Nicci Jordan, Arvid Wallen, Kathy Mosier, Pat Reinheimer

Printed in Canada

1 2 3 4 5 6 7 8 9 10 / 09 08 07 06 05

CONTENTS

INTRODUCTION

And now for something completely different . . .

You know what to expect in a devotion.

A little Bible verse.
A little story.
A little prayer.
A little time with God.

You can zip through it in less time than it takes for your bowl of Cap'n Crunch to become Cap'n Mushy after you pour in the milk.

As soon as you turn the page, you may think this devotion is no different. After all, it won't bombard you with a ton of words on every page. You can read each of these seventy devotions in about seven minutes or less. Hence the title, 7 Minutes with Jesus.

But this book in your hands is not the same-old, same-old. For one thing, the devotions don't start with you. They start with God. Each week you will explore a different aspect of the character of God the Son, Jesus Christ. For another thing, each week is put together so that no two days are alike. On the first day, you will read the Bible to get you thinking about the topic for the week. Another day you will focus on prayer. Another on praise. Another on taking action based on what you've read. You'll even be challenged to fast once a week, but no two fasts are alike. Skipping a meal or two is just one way to do it.

Each week also includes a reflection on the week's topic by a student from Azusa Pacific University. These students have put on paper some of the things you think but never believed anyone would put into words. They have also written many of the other daily devotions. To learn more about these students, check out the contributors section at the end of the book.

The final devotion each week is primarily a bunch of blank lines waiting for your writing. We didn't run out of things to say and therefore decide to use the lines to fill space. The lines are there for you to journal your thoughts from the week. As you consider the character of Jesus, what do you want to say to Him in response? Tell Him in this journaling section.

We didn't write this devotion to give you seventy pithy thoughts. Instead, we want your Bible reading and prayer and fasts to be launching points for conversations between you and God that last much longer than seven minutes each. Our goal is to help you think through your faith. In the end, as you come to see your faith through God's eyes, we hope the way you see your world changes.

This devotion is different. It is different by design. And by the time you get to the end, we pray you will be different too.

Mark Tabb, general editor

GOD IN FLESH

//JOHN 1:1-14

The Word was first,
   the Word present to God,
   God present to the Word.
The Word was God,
   in readiness for God from
      day one.

Everything was created
      through him;
   nothing—not one
      thing!—
   came into being without
      him.
What came into existence
      was Life,
   and the Life was Light to
      live by.
The Life-Light blazed out of
      the darkness;
   the darkness couldn't put
      it out.

There once was a man, his name
John, sent by God to point out
the way to the Life-Light. He
came to show everyone where
to look, who to believe in. John
was not himself the Light; he
was there to show the way to
the Light.

The Life-Light was the real
      thing:
   Every person entering Life
   he brings into Light.
He was in the world,
   the world was there
      through him,
   and yet the world didn't
      even notice.
He came to his own people,
   but they didn't want him.
But whoever did want him,
   who believed he was who
      he claimed
   and would do what he
      said,
He made to be their true
      selves,

BIBLE READING

their child-of-God selves.
These are the God-begotten,
    not blood-begotten,
    not flesh-begotten,
    not sex-begotten.

The Word became flesh and
    blood,
    and moved into the
        neighborhood.
We saw the glory with our
        own eyes,
    the one-of-a-kind glory,
    like Father, like Son,
Generous inside and out,
    true from start to finish.

The entire Christian faith starts here: God became flesh and blood and came to earth. Jesus, the Word, was God. He made everything in the universe. Then He came to this earth He made, but no one noticed Him. He came to His own, but instead of welcoming Him, they killed Him. Fortunately for us, He didn't stay dead. God in flesh and blood rose again on the third day. This is Christianity 101.

Everything we take for granted about our relationship with God comes down to this truth. Before you pass by too quickly, ask yourself, *Why would God go through all of this for me? Why would He leave heaven and come down here to die? What could He possibly gain that would make the pain worth it?*

GOD IN FLESH

EXODUS 3:13-14

Then Moses said to God, "Suppose I go to the People of Israel and I tell them, 'The God of your fathers sent me to you'; and they ask me, 'What is his name?' What do I tell them?"

God said to Moses, "I-AM-WHO-I-AM. Tell the People of Israel, 'I-AM sent me to you.'"

JOHN 8:57-59

The Jews said, "You're not even fifty years old—and Abraham saw you?"

"Believe me," said Jesus, "*I am who I am* long before Abraham was anything."

That did it—pushed them over the edge. They picked up rocks to throw at him. But Jesus slipped away, getting out of the Temple.

PRAYER & SOLITUDE

//PRAY

Have you ever tried to pray as if you were talking to God in the flesh? How do you think this would change how you structured your prayer? Today, try to pray as if you were having a conversation with a fellow human being. Talk to Jesus as someone who has walked in your shoes and experienced what you've experienced. Not only did He walk in the flesh in the past, but He also walks next to us each day. He's been here in the flesh, and He's here now in the Spirit. Talk to Him as if you're talking to your best friend. He can identify with you, and He understands what you're going through.

Annie Moddelmog
Age: 21
Major: nursing

//REFLECT

Sometimes I struggle with prayer. God seems so far away and inaccessible. I know He sees what is going on in my life, but can He really identify with me? Does He really know what it is like to deal with the day-to-day issues I deal with? Then I read the Bible, and I discover that the mighty God who talked to Moses in the burning bush is the same God who put on flesh and blood and came to earth. Jesus came down to earth and walked among people like us. He hung out with those who were rejected by society. Knowing that God was in the flesh can help us to better identify with Him.

GOD IN FLESH

//PHILIPPIANS 2:5-8

Think of yourselves the way Christ Jesus thought of himself. He had equal status with God but didn't think so much of himself that he had to cling to the advantages of that status no matter what. Not at all. When the time came, he set aside the privileges of deity and took on the status of a slave, became *human*! Having become human, he stayed human. It was an incredibly humbling process. He didn't claim special privileges. Instead, he lived a selfless, obedient life and then died a selfless, obedient death—and the worst kind of death at that: a crucifixion.

//REFLECT

Often I get so busy with accomplishing my everyday tasks that I can't see anything else. Living due date to due date (with projects, papers, tests, and so on) leaves little time for anything else. Sometimes I step back and ask myself, *Is there something more to this life?*

I find my answer in Jesus. Even though He was fully God, He didn't go around bragging about it. Instead, He served others. He loved them unconditionally and invested His life in them, despite the fact that doing so led to His death. He did all this to be obedient to His Father, not to feel good about Himself.

FASTING

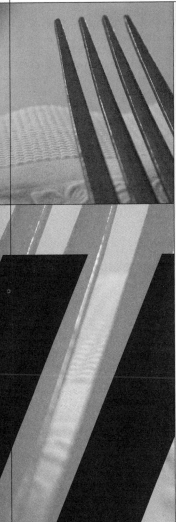

//FAST

Jesus served others, and if we're serious about being His followers, we should imitate His actions. Therefore, take a "time" fast today. Don't use your time for yourself; instead, donate it by serving others. Don't pick some quick and easy task you can do in a couple of minutes, such as carrying someone's tray in the cafeteria. Pick a task that demands enough time that it completely changes your schedule for the day. While you're serving, focus on the needs of others and not your own. Love people the way Christ loves us. Let the words of Philippians 2:5-8 be your motivation and guide for how to serve selflessly as Jesus did. Bless someone with your time, and you in turn will be greatly blessed.

Emily Penner
Age: 20
Major: nursing

GOD IN FLESH

ACTION

//MATTHEW 6:14-15; 18:21-22

MATTHEW 6:14-15

"In prayer there is a connection between what God does and what you do. You can't get forgiveness from God, for instance, without also forgiving others. If you refuse to do your part, you cut yourself off from God's part."

MATTHEW 18:21-22

At that point Peter got up the nerve to ask, "Master, how many times do I forgive a brother or sister who hurts me? Seven?"

Jesus replied, "Seven! Hardly. Try seventy times seven."

//REFLECT

When I look back at my life, there are thousands of things I wish I could forget. Some of those things are known by others, and some I keep to myself. My life has been filled with struggles to stay away from sin, and many times I've failed. The only thing I know, the only thing that keeps me from hating myself, is that God loves me and has forgiven me. I didn't deserve it; God gave it to me as a gift. Jesus came to earth in human flesh to receive the punishment that everyone deserves. None of us is perfect, but we have been made perfect through Jesus. He lived here on earth so that He could know everything we go through in life. Being perfect, He was able to withstand the tests we endure every day. Then He gave His life as a payment for our sins. Now, through the salvation He has given to us, we no longer have to suffer the death that we deserved. We have been forgiven.

//ACT

Receiving forgiveness from God is only half of the equation. We must forgive others because God forgives us for both big and small things. Pay close attention to the small things that get on your nerves, like the guy who cut you off in traffic or your little brother who borrowed your iPod without asking. Instead of losing your cool with people, immediately forgive them. That's how God treats us. When we pass His forgiveness on to others, we help them see how real God is.

Jessica Meydag
Age: 23
Major: nursing

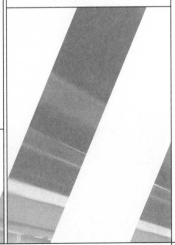

GOD IN FLESH

//COLOSSIANS 1:18-20

[Jesus] was supreme in the beginning and—leading the resurrection parade—he is supreme in the end. From beginning to end he's there, towering far above everything, everyone. So spacious is he, so roomy, that everything of God finds its proper place in him without crowding. Not only that, but all the broken and dislocated pieces of the universe—people and things, animals and atoms—get properly fixed and fit together in vibrant harmonies, all because of his death, his blood that poured down from the Cross.

PRAISE & CELEBRATION

//REFLECT

I have never understood why God would take on human flesh for a sinner like me. I constantly struggle with accepting His acceptance of me. I live in fear—fear of failure and fear of rejection. Every day I wonder how everyone else seems to always have it all together, while I feel totally screwed up. I often think, *I am not worthy of God's love.*

But this passage reminds me that God took on human flesh so I can be free—free from comparisons to others, free from my sin, and free from the fear that so often drives me. My life is one of the broken and dislocated pieces of the universe the cross puts back together. I understand this with my mind, but my heart doesn't always feel it. I know I'm not alone. I wonder why my heart is always the hardest to convince.

//PRAISE

Rather than waiting for your heart to feel God's truth, start in your mind with what you know: Jesus became human *for you.* Praise Him for the hope He gives in the midst of your daily struggles. Celebrate the fact that this world is not eternal, that God has a new world waiting for you, a world filled with love and acceptance. Stop putting stock in the opinions of fellow sinners and praise God for what He says about you. Let praise dissolve your fears today as you stand in awe at the foot of the cross.

Katrina Anker
Age: 20
Major: nursing

GOD IN FLESH

//MY FOCUS: HEBREWS 2:14-18

Since the children are made of flesh and blood, it's logical that the Savior took on flesh and blood in order to rescue them by his death. By embracing death, taking it into himself, he destroyed the Devil's hold on death and freed all who cower through life, scared to death of death.

It's obvious, of course, that he didn't go to all this trouble for angels. It was for people like us, children of Abraham. That's why he had to enter into every detail of human life. Then, when he came before God as high priest to get rid of the people's sins, he would have already experienced it all himself—all the pain, all the testing—and would be able to help where help was needed.

MY JOURNEY

//MY GOD

I am one of those people who cower through life "scared to death of death." I cower in my fear of the future, of criticism, of failure, of being unloved. I don't always act like I'm scared or even think about it that often. But it's always there in the back of my mind. When I'm alone and the noise of my music, television, and instant messenger have ceased, these thoughts silently push their way forward.

And to think I'm frightened of these things when You, Jesus, came and conquered death, the greatest fear of all! You didn't face death as an all-powerful God but chose to face it as I will someday: in human flesh. How much more can You free me from my fears when I am reminded that You faced the same ones and more—and conquered them all?

Remembering Your life and death puts my troubles into perspective. How can I ever feel unloved or ignored when I remember that I am more precious than angels in Your eyes?

//MY PRAYER

Jesus, thank You for leaving the glory of heaven just to come here and die for a sinner like me. I pray that I would remember the sacrifice You made and never take it for granted. I pray that I would remember that You lived like me in human flesh and that You understand all of my hopes, dreams, and fears. I pray that I would gain strength and courage to face each day, knowing that You had the power to overcome death. Help me to know just how precious I am to You.

Amy Rice
Age: 21
Major: nursing

//JOURNALING: 1 JOHN 5:20-21

And we know that the Son of God came so we could recognize and understand the truth of God—what a gift!—and we are living in the Truth itself, in God's Son, Jesus Christ. This Jesus is both True God and Real Life. Dear children, be on guard against all clever facsimiles.

Six days ago you were asked to consider why Jesus would take on flesh and come to earth to suffer for you. Before you move on, you need to wrestle with another question, a question that cannot be answered with words alone: Now what? The Son of God came so you can recognize and understand the truth of God. Now what will you do with it?

SERVANT KING

// PSALM 2 AND MARK 10:42-45

PSALM 2

Why the big noise, nations?
Why the mean plots,
	peoples?
Earth-leaders push for
	position,
Demagogues and delegates
	meet for summit talks,
The God-deniers, the
	Messiah-defiers:
"Let's get free of God!
Cast loose from Messiah!"
Heaven-throned God breaks
	out laughing.
At first he's amused at their
	presumption;
Then he gets good and
	angry.
Furiously, he shuts them up:
"Don't you know there's
	a King in Zion? A
	coronation banquet
Is spread for him on the holy
	summit."

Let me tell you what GOD
	said next.
He said, "You're my son,
And today is your birthday.
What do you want? Name it:
Nations as a present?
	continents as a prize?
You can command them all
	to dance for you,
Or throw them out with
	tomorrow's trash."

So, rebel-kings, use your
	heads;
Upstart-judges, learn your
	lesson:
Worship GOD in adoring
	embrace,
Celebrate in trembling awe.
	Kiss Messiah!
Your very lives are in danger,
	you know;
His anger is about to
	explode,

BIBLE READING

But if you make a run for
God—you won't regret
it!

MARK 10:42-45

Jesus got them together to settle things down. "You've observed how godless rulers throw their weight around," he said, "and when people get a little power how quickly it goes to their heads. It's not going to be that way with you. Whoever wants to be great must become a servant. Whoever wants to be first among you must be your slave. That is what the Son of Man has done: He came to serve, not to be served—and then to give away his life in exchange for many who are held hostage."

//REFLECT

Both of these passages describe Jesus. He is the Messiah seated on heaven's throne who can command all the kings of the earth to dance before Him, yet He came to earth as a humble servant. The One who could throw all the nations out with the trash instead washed His disciples' crud-encrusted feet. This week we will stand in awe of our King's example. As we do, we will hear Him calling us to do what He did. Although we will one day rule with Him in heaven, we are to become servants in this world today.

SERVANT KING

He was looked down on and
   passed over,
   a man who suffered, who
      knew pain firsthand.
One look at him and people
   turned away.
   We looked down on him,
      thought he was scum.
But the fact is, it was *our*
   pains he carried —
   our disfigurements, all the
      things wrong with *us*.
We thought he brought it on
   himself,
   that God was punishing
      him for his own
      failures.
But it was our sins that did
   that to him,
that ripped and tore and
   crushed him — *our sins*!
He took the punishment, and
   that made us whole.
Through his bruises we get
   healed.

MY JOURNEY

//MY GOD

My parents divorced when I was in kindergarten. My mother received custody of me; my father got custody of my sister. Although I still had enforced visits with my father, I never felt welcomed by him since he had fought for the custody of my sister and not for me. As a little girl, I dreamed that I would have a normal family again. As soon as I had begun to adjust to my situation, my dreams were shattered again.

On my way home from a vacation with my sister and father during the summer before fifth grade, my father stopped at the terminal and told me, "You are going home alone, and you will probably never see me or your sister again." I was a strong girl. I boarded my plane destined for life without my father and sister. Even though I reconnected with them five years later, the time in between was hard to overcome. I lived with my own self-pity. I cried out to God, "How could you do this to me? Why me after all I have been through?" I never doubted God's existence, but I did doubt His love.

After lots of time, I have begun to understand that Jesus felt my pain before I even endured it. I finally realize that I am not alone in the world. The King died for my sins—all of them, including my self-pity. I will never feel pain that is too great for Him. On the cross, He bore my pain multiplied by the sorrows of the entire world. Clearly, Jesus really does love me.

//MY PRAYER

I pray that I would see my own self-pity fade away as I focus on Christ's sufferings. When I feel alone in my sorrows, help me to remember that it was my pains He carried before I even knew that pain existed. May I wake up every day praising God for the good things He has done in my life. God, please replace my self-pity with the overwhelming and sacrificial love of Christ who loves me and gave Himself for me.

Susanna R. Eskridge
Age: 19
Major: communications

SERVANT KING

//PHILIPPIANS 3:8-9

Yes, all the things I once thought were so important are gone from my life. Compared to the high privilege of knowing Christ Jesus as my Master, firsthand, everything I once thought I had going for me is insignificant—dog dung. I've dumped it all in the trash so that I could embrace Christ and be embraced by him.

//REFLECT

I often question my decisions in the relationships I have with members of the opposite sex. At times, I find myself in situations that not only jeopardize everything that I stand for—purity, truth, and honor—but also distract me from hearing God calling me to Himself. In an effort to look sexy or hot, I often behave immodestly. The way I dress attracts attention, but it is not the eyes of God that look at me. I crave the looks I get from guys because they make me feel better about myself. Why do I do this?

FASTING

//FAST

This week, take a relationship fast in order that you may better serve God. Don't fill yourself with empty love that is not pure and honest. Instead, empty yourself just as Jesus Christ did. Take a break from (and actually break yourself from) any relationship that is coming between you and God. During this time, when you feel alone and lost, do not pick up the phone to call your friends or rush to the computer to chat online. Instead, turn to your Lord who stands with open arms. Lean on Him alone. He accepts you just as you are. Cling to Him. After the fast is over, work to form relationships with others that reflect a passion for God and a desire to serve Him.

Jessica van der Stad
Age: 19
Major: communications with an
    emphasis in journalism

Grabbing attention feels so important until I look at Jesus. He is always there, even when I cling to the arm of someone who looks at me with impure thoughts. The Lord still stands beside me, loving me through my mistakes and pulling me closer to Him. Compared to the high privilege of knowing Him, no other relationship matters. He is the One I need above everyone else.

SERVANT KING

//PHILIPPIANS 2:5-6

Think of yourselves the way Christ Jesus thought of himself. He had equal status with God but didn't think so much of himself that he had to cling to the advantages of that status no matter what.

//REFLECT

If we aren't careful, we Christians can automatically assume that being saved makes us better than everyone else. We get used to living in God's fold, and we start looking down on the lost. Throw in the Bible's promises about going to heaven and reigning with Christ, and we start to feel like we are among the elite. I know I sometimes fall into the trap of thinking so highly of myself that I forget God has called me to the humble life of a servant.

PRAYER & SOLITUDE

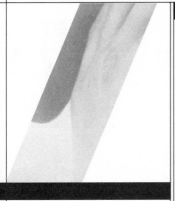

Jesus knew His status, but He did not allow that to get in the way of serving others. If we want to be like Christ, we must be willing to lay aside our egos and allow ourselves to be humbled into the position of a servant. Think about your motives when you're witnessing to others. Do you really want them to develop a relationship with Christ, or are you playing the numbers game ("I've led twenty-five people to Christ! How about you?")? What's really important is that Christ not only *lived* a servant life but also *died* a servant death. Are you allowing God to use you as a servant?

//PRAY

Every one of Christ's followers is adopted royalty, but being royalty does not mean that we cannot serve others or that we are better than others. Start your time of prayer by listening to God. Think about the various ways Christ allowed Himself to be used as a Servant King. Look up some passages that talk about that and pay close attention to the ways He served and how He related to the people He was serving. Then ask God to change your heart and make you a servant. Humble yourself and ask Him to make this servant mentality permeate your heart and mind. Don't stop there. Pray for God to show you ways that you can serve Him by serving others. Ask Him to open your eyes to those He wants to touch through you. Remember, when you serve others, you are really serving God. He will reward you for your efforts.

Carissa Sechrist
Age: 21
Major: communications

SERVANT KING

ACTION

//MARK 2:15-17

Later Jesus and his disciples were at home having supper with a collection of disreputable guests. Unlikely as it seems, more than a few of them had become followers. The religion scholars and Pharisees saw him keeping this kind of company and lit into his disciples: "What kind of example is this, acting cozy with the riff-raff?"

Jesus, overhearing, shot back, "Who needs a doctor: the healthy or the sick? I'm here inviting the sin-sick, not the spiritually-fit."

//ACT

Think of a person at your school or church or on your athletic team who most people look down on or never pay any attention to. Go to her and make her feel loved and appreciated. Serve her. Help her out in any way you can. Sit with her at lunch, talk to her, help her with her homework, offer her a soda. God will bless you for this courageous act that has the power to put a smile on a face and maybe even change a life!

Warning: Today's action has to last longer than one day. Don't act like you genuinely care for someone today and then ignore him tomorrow. Serving the outcasts was Jesus' way of life, not a mission project He did once in a while. If you are serious about following His example, it must become a way of life for you as well.

Jenna Willems
Age: 20
Major: communications with an
    emphasis in interpersonal/
    organizational; cognate in marketing/
    business

//REFLECT

God gave Jesus the throne of the world, yet He hung out with the lowliest people. He treated "riff-raff" like they were high and mighty. He took the time to connect with people who didn't seem like His kind. By showing love, compassion, grace, and mercy, He mirrored the heart of His Father. He didn't care what the religion scholars thought; He cared only about what His Father thought. His actions are the example we're to follow.

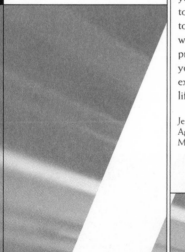

SERVANT KING

//ISAIAH 53:7-10

He was beaten, he was
    tortured,
    but he didn't say a word.
Like a lamb taken to be
    slaughtered
    and like a sheep being
    sheared,
    he took it all in silence.
Justice miscarried, and he
    was led off—
    and did anyone really
    know what was
    happening?
He died without a thought
    for his own welfare,
    beaten bloody for the sins
    of my people.
They buried him with the
    wicked,
threw him in a grave with
    a rich man,
Even though he'd never hurt
    a soul
    or said one word that
    wasn't true.

Still, it's what GOD had in
    mind all along,
    to crush him with pain.
The plan was that he give
    himself as an offering
    for sin
    so that he'd see life come
    from it—life, life, and
    more life.
And GOD's plan will deeply
    prosper through him.

PRAISE & CELEBRATION

//REFLECT

Sometimes I think I've sacrificed a lot for God. Then I look at Jesus. Jesus gave up more than swearing or gossip. He didn't just vow to honor His mother and father or promise to go to church every Sunday or simply help the poor in His own town. He actually gave His life. He made the greatest sacrifice a human could give in exchange for our lives.

Because He was fully human, Jesus got frustrated. He got tired. He was tempted. He could have given up at any moment and escaped a greater physical pain than I can even begin to imagine. But He didn't. Instead, He sacrificed His life for the sake of God's plan. He gave His life for you and me without even a thought of His own welfare. The King came and served, even though it cost Him His life.

//PRAISE

Praise God today by sacrificing to Him all your expectations of Him. Instead of focusing on giving up little things like swearing and gossip, go a step further. Worship Him by releasing the worldly desires that get in the way of His eternal plan. Do this for the sake of His plan. Write them down on a piece of paper and then offer them up to God as an act of worship. Pray over each desire, praising Him for all that He has sacrificed. As you pray, rip off a piece of the paper until it's all in the garbage, symbolizing your own personal sacrifice of praise.

Crissa Nelson
Age: 18
Major: journalism

//JOURNALING: LUKE 22:24-27

Within minutes they were bickering over who of them would end up the greatest. But Jesus intervened: "Kings like to throw their weight around and people in authority like to give themselves fancy titles. It's not going to be that way with you. Let the senior among you become like the junior; let the leader act the part of the servant.

"Who would you rather be: the one who eats the dinner or the one who serves the dinner? You'd rather eat and be served, right? But I've taken my place among you as the one who serves."

Becoming a servant is never easy, but we have no other choice. What changes do you need to make in your life to become a servant like Jesus?

COUNTERCULTURAL

//MATTHEW 5:2-12

This is what [Jesus] said:

"You're blessed when you're at the end of your rope. With less of you there is more of God and his rule.

"You're blessed when you feel you've lost what is most dear to you. Only then can you be embraced by the One most dear to you.

"You're blessed when you're content with just who you are—no more, no less. That's the moment you find yourselves proud owners of everything that can't be bought.

"You're blessed when you've worked up a good appetite for God. He's food and drink in the best meal you'll ever eat.

"You're blessed when you care. At the moment of being 'care-full,' you find yourselves cared for.

"You're blessed when you get your inside world—your mind and heart—put right. Then you can see God in the outside world.

"You're blessed when you can show people how to cooperate instead of compete or fight. That's when you discover who you really are, and your place in God's family.

"You're blessed when your commitment to God provokes persecution. The persecution drives you even deeper into God's kingdom.

BIBLE READING

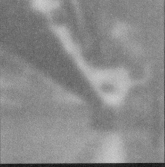

"Not only that—count yourselves blessed every time people put you down or throw you out or speak lies about you to discredit me. What it means is that the truth is too close for comfort and they are uncomfortable. You can be glad when that happens—give a cheer, even!—for though they don't like it, *I* do! And all heaven applauds. And know that you are in good company. My prophets and witnesses have always gotten into this kind of trouble."

//REFLECT

Jesus' words are backward. They stand the world system on its head. Jesus didn't shape His message for popularity. He went against the tide with both the religious and secular leaders of His day. That's why they killed Him. What does it mean to follow a countercultural Savior in the twenty-first century? You will find out as we spend a week looking at the Sermon on the Mount.

COUNTERCULTURAL

//MATTHEW 5:27-29

"You know the next commandment pretty well, too: 'Don't go to bed with another's spouse.' But don't think you've preserved your virtue simply by staying out of bed. Your *heart* can be corrupted by lust even quicker than your *body*. Those leering looks you think nobody notices—they also corrupt.

"Let's not pretend this is easier than it really is. If you want to live a morally pure life, here's what you have to do: You have to blind your right eye the moment you catch it in a lustful leer. You have to choose to live one-eyed or else be dumped on a moral trash pile."

//REFLECT

Obviously Jesus didn't live in the twenty-first century. Keeping the eye away from sexually charged material may have been easy in His day, but it sure isn't today. Sexual references are everywhere. I came across an ad for gum that used a double meaning to suggest both the need for chewing gum and sex. If we take Jesus' words literally, we're all going to end up walking around without right eyes—or, for that matter, left ones. Yet keeping the heart free from lust has never been easy, today or two thousand years ago. Jesus isn't only telling us not to obsess over sex. He is telling us that real purity goes beyond signing a True Love Waits card. We have to guard our hearts no matter the cost.

FASTING

//THE NEXT LEVEL

At the end of the fast, look back on the volume of stuff you had to avoid. Was it more or less than you thought it would be? Since Jesus' words apply to more than just one day, what kinds of changes do you need to make in your daily lifestyle to make His words a permanent part of your life?

//FAST

You don't have to pluck out your eye to keep today's fast, but you will need to take some drastic steps. Your assignment won't be easy. Today, fast from anything that tries to stir up lust inside of you. Obviously, pornography or sexually explicit movies are out. You also need to separate yourself from television shows, movies, music, magazines, or anything else that makes sex outside of marriage look like no big deal. Avoid people who talk about their sexual exploits and do not wear anything that might stir up lust in someone else. Ask God to make you hyperaware of all the sexually suggestive materials that surround you and then separate yourself from them.

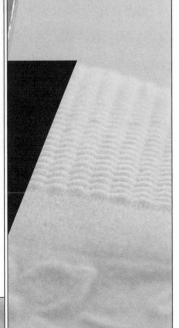

COUNTERCULTURAL

ACTION

//MATTHEW 5:43-48

"You're familiar with the old written law, 'Love your friend,' and its unwritten companion, 'Hate your enemy.' I'm challenging that. I'm telling you to love your enemies. Let them bring out the best in you, not the worst. When someone gives you a hard time, respond with the energies of prayer, for then you are working out of your true selves, your God-created selves. This is what God does. He gives his best—the sun to warm and the rain to nourish—to everyone, regardless: the good and bad, the nice and nasty. If all you do is love the lovable, do you expect a bonus? Anybody can do that. If you simply say hello to those who greet you, do you expect a medal? Any run-of-the-mill sinner does that.

"In a word, what I'm saying is, *Grow up*. You're kingdom subjects. Now live like it. Live out your God-created identity. Live generously and graciously toward others, the way God lives toward you."

//ACT

Today, find a person you have been fighting with or a person you don't get along with. Ask him what you can do for him or how you can help him. Put Jesus' words into action by making yourself available to him. Also, don't expect him to be so overcome by your act of kindness that the two of you suddenly become best friends. He might laugh in your face and tell you to get lost. Or he might take advantage of you and ask you to do some gross, grimy task just to see how serious you are. If he does, how will you respond?

John Gaquin
Age: 23
Major: communications

//REFLECT

How should we treat people who do us wrong? Jesus gives an answer we don't expect. He goes completely against the flow and tells us to do the exact opposite of what we want to do. Instead of getting even, He tells us to be a servant. Instead of paying back evil for evil, He tells us to do good to those who do bad to us.

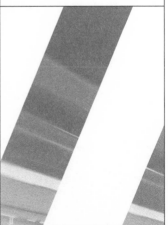

COUNTERCULTURAL

//MATTHEW 6:5-8

"And when you come before God, don't turn that into a theatrical production either. All these people making a regular show out of their prayers, hoping for stardom! Do you think God sits in a box seat?

"Here's what I want you to do: Find a quiet, secluded place so you won't be tempted to role-play before God. Just be there as simply and honestly as you can manage. The focus will shift from you to God, and you will begin to sense his grace.

"The world is full of so-called prayer warriors who are prayer-ignorant. They're full of formulas and programs and advice, peddling techniques for getting what you want from God. Don't fall for that nonsense. This is your Father you are dealing with, and he knows better than you what you need."

PRAYER & SOLITUDE

//REFLECT

Ever heard a really good prayer? You know, the kind that's obviously been rehearsed fifty times, just to make sure it sounds good. The kind that could win an Academy Award for best presentation, maybe even best picture. Beautiful language. Flowing rhythm. And the perfect words to fill the audience with overwhelming joy or repentant tears.

Wait a minute. What audience?

We live in a society so obsessed with appearances that we sometimes forget God knows what's beneath the costume. We want our ratings to go up, so we develop the perfect spiritual life to catch the attention of God and anyone else who might be listening. But God knows what's really going on, and the act doesn't impress Him. All He wants is a real conversation between Him and us. He has a lot to say, but we won't hear it through the practiced lines.

//PRAY

Take a few minutes today to reflect on the God you've been praying to. What is He like? Think for a minute about why you are praying. Prayer isn't about talking *at* God but *to* Him, *with* Him. When you pray, you're talking to Someone who is real, Someone who is actually listening, Someone who knows your heart and not just your words.

Next, just start talking. It doesn't matter if you start with "Dear God" or end with "Amen." Tell God what's in your heart. There is no secret prayer formula, and you're not going to lose a grade or win an award for your form. Skip the structure and just talk to God like the close friend He wants to be.

Hannah Kelmis
Age: 22
Major: English

COUNTERCULTURAL

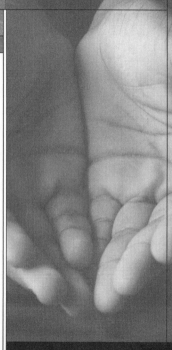

//MATTHEW 6:28-31

"All this time and money wasted on fashion—do you think it makes that much difference? Instead of looking at the fashions, walk out into the fields and look at the wildflowers. They never primp or shop, but have you ever seen color and design quite like it? The ten best-dressed men and women in the country look shabby alongside them.

"If God gives such attention to the appearance of wildflowers—most of which are never even seen—don't you think he'll attend to you, take pride in you, do his best for you? What I'm trying to do here is to get you to relax, to not be so preoccupied with *getting*, so you can respond to God's *giving*."

PRAISE & CELEBRATION

//REFLECT

Jesus essentially says worrying about money and possessions is a total waste. I love the way *The Message* puts the last verse. Instead of being preoccupied with getting, Jesus wants us to relax so we can respond to all God gives us. He will make sure we have what we need. If that is true, and it is, why do we worry? Instead, we should focus on God and His kingdom, figuring out how we can serve Him rather than trying to find a way to get the latest fashion, CD, computer, or whatever gets your "I've got to have it" motor running.

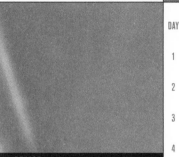

//PRAISE

The best way to show we're taking Jesus' words on money seriously is to turn loose some of it. Give God an offering of some of your hard-earned cash. Make this both a true act of faith and an act of worship. Don't give grudgingly or look at this as a down payment on some special blessing from God. Give an amount that forces you to trust God, but not so much that you start patting yourself on the back for your generosity. Give out of joy. If possible, give anonymously so that no one knows what you've done except you and God.

COUNTERCULTURAL

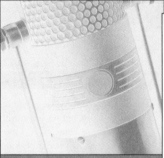

//MY FOCUS: MATTHEW 7:13-14

"Don't look for shortcuts to God. The market is flooded with surefire, easygoing formulas for a successful life that can be practiced in your spare time. Don't fall for that stuff, even though crowds of people do. The way to life—to God!—is vigorous and requires total attention."

MY JOURNEY

//MY GOD

I don't want to play church anymore. It seems easy enough to bring my Bible to church with me on Sundays, while the rest of the week it gathers dust on the bookshelf. I'm not a saint, but I do desire to live with a sense of purpose. Otherwise, what's the sense in living? Still, I'll admit that sometimes I don't want to read it.

And this affects my prayer life. Some nights I find that my prayers consist of meaningless wants rather than listening in silence for what God desires to tell me. In many ways, I try to come to

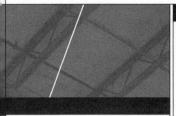

God on my own terms rather than His. I forget that He has a purpose for my life that really *is* in my best interest. I don't know what it is, but I'm going to find out. To do that, I need to listen to God and not drown Him out with my list of demands. I know the Christian life isn't supposed to be easy, but oftentimes it is downright difficult.

//MY PRAYER

How can I please You if I never have time to talk to You? But even if there were enough hours in the day, I would still get distracted by things that won't matter in the long run.

I pray that I would live in such a way that my life would reflect the inner workings of Your love and mercy. You don't expect me to be perfect, which is good because I never will be no matter how hard I try. Rather than complain about how difficult life may seem, I want to be reminded of Your promise to never let me fall out of Your love. And if I mess up, I know You will be there to encourage me.

//MY THOUGHTS

- What does it mean to listen to God?
- What areas in my life can God improve if I let Him?
- How will God reveal His purpose for my life?

Henry Romero
Age: 21
Major: English

//JOURNALING: MATTHEW 7:24-27

"These words I speak to you are not incidental additions to your life, homeowner improvements to your standard of living. They are foundational words, words to build a life on. If you work these words into your life, you are like a smart carpenter who built his house on solid rock. Rain poured down, the river flooded, a tornado hit—but nothing moved that house. It was fixed to the rock.

"But if you just use my words in Bible studies and don't work them into your life, you are like a stupid carpenter who built his house on the sandy beach. When a storm rolled in and the waves came up, it collapsed like a house of cards."

How are you going to build your life on what you've read this week?

UNPREDICTABLE

A man was sick, Lazarus of Bethany, the town of Mary and her sister Martha. This was the same Mary who massaged the Lord's feet with aromatic oils and then wiped them with her hair. It was her brother Lazarus who was sick. So the sisters sent word to Jesus, "Master, the one you love so very much is sick."

When Jesus got the message, he said, "This sickness is not fatal. It will become an occasion to show God's glory by glorifying God's Son."

Jesus loved Martha and her sister and Lazarus, but oddly, when he heard that Lazarus was sick, he stayed on where he was for two more days. . . .

When Jesus finally got there, he found Lazarus already four days dead. Bethany was near Jerusalem, only a couple of miles away, and many of the Jews were visiting Martha and Mary, sympathizing with them over their brother. Martha heard Jesus was coming and went out to meet him. Mary remained in the house.

Martha said, "Master, if you'd been here, my brother wouldn't have died. Even now, I know that whatever you ask God he will give you."

Jesus said, "Your brother will be raised up."

Martha replied, "I know that he will be raised up in the resurrection at the end of time."

"You don't have to wait for the End. I am, right now,

BIBLE READING

Resurrection and Life. The one who believes in me, even though he or she dies, will live. And everyone who lives believing in me does not ultimately die at all. Do you believe this?"

"Yes, Master. All along I have believed that you are the Messiah, the Son of God who comes into the world."

After saying this, she went to her sister Mary and whispered in her ear, "The Teacher is here and is asking for you."

The moment she heard that, she jumped up and ran out to him.

//REFLECT

Put yourself in Martha's and Mary's sandals. They could not understand why Jesus didn't get there faster. Why did Jesus wait? Why didn't He come and fix the situation before it was too late? This wasn't the only time Jesus surprised people by not doing what they expected. He delighted in doing the unexpected. Since He doesn't change, we can count on Him being unpredictable in our lives today. How will that affect your relationship with Him?

UNPREDICTABLE

//JOHN 20:3-9

Peter and the other disciple left immediately for the tomb. They ran, neck and neck. The other disciple got to the tomb first, outrunning Peter. Stooping to look in, he saw the pieces of linen cloth lying there, but he didn't go in. Simon Peter arrived after him, entered the tomb, observed the linen cloths lying there, and the kerchief used to cover his head not lying with the linen cloths but separate, neatly folded by itself. Then the other disciple, the one who had gotten there first, went into the tomb, took one look at the evidence, and believed. No one yet knew from the Scripture that he had to rise from the dead.

PRAISE & CELEBRATION

//REFLECT

During the summer after my senior year in high school, I was trying to decide whether to go to junior college for a semester or to study in the Sierra Nevada mountains in a program sponsored by a university. My mom made the decision for me, which made me furious. Not only did I not get to decide where I wanted to attend school, but I had to live in the woods for three months. Summer ended, and I began my three months of "boot camp." To my surprise, Christ had more in store for me than I was ready for. In those three months, I was pushed physically, mentally, and spiritually through backpacking, strenuous academics, and a broken heart. That semester changed my life completely; I left a different person. I never expected what God did.

Jesus' disciples didn't understand why He had to die until He rose again. Then their anger and grief turned into joy. That's how I felt at the end of my semester in the mountains. When God acts in unpredictable ways, you don't know what He is really up to until the end.

//PRAISE

Make a list of all the times your plans didn't turn out the way you wanted or expected. Include those times that made you mad because you wanted your life to go in a different direction. Then go back over the list and look for ways God worked in those situations, especially the ones you didn't want to be in to begin with. How did He shape your life? How is your life different today because you went through those situations? Spend time praising God for working in unpredictable ways in your life. Thank Him even if you cannot yet see how He is going to use what you are going through.

Lindsey Rinehart
Age: 19
Major: undeclared (focused toward nutrition or athletic training)

UNPREDICTABLE

//MATTHEW 14:28-31

Peter, suddenly bold, said, "Master, if it's really you, call me to come to you on the water."

He said, "Come ahead."

Jumping out of the boat, Peter walked on the water to Jesus. But when he looked down at the waves churning beneath his feet, he lost his nerve and started to sink. He cried, "Master, save me!"

Jesus didn't hesitate. He reached down and grabbed his hand. Then he said, "Faint-heart, what got into you?"

//REFLECT

My father left my family when I was in eighth grade. And since, it has seemed impossible to restore that relationship. But the word *impossible* is not in Jesus' vocabulary. No matter how hard a relationship or situation may seem, God can do what we think is incomprehensible. Too often I'm like Peter. I start looking at the wind and waves, and doubt overtakes me. But even when he started to sink, Peter knew he could call out for help and Jesus would be there. Jesus will be there in my relationship with my father, and He will be there for everything else.

FASTING

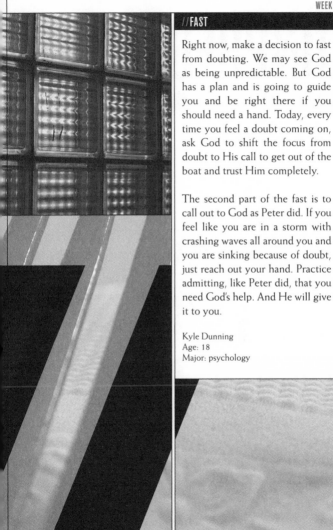

//FAST

Right now, make a decision to fast from doubting. We may see God as being unpredictable. But God has a plan and is going to guide you and be right there if you should need a hand. Today, every time you feel a doubt coming on, ask God to shift the focus from doubt to His call to get out of the boat and trust Him completely.

The second part of the fast is to call out to God as Peter did. If you feel like you are in a storm with crashing waves all around you and you are sinking because of doubt, just reach out your hand. Practice admitting, like Peter did, that you need God's help. And He will give it to you.

Kyle Dunning
Age: 18
Major: psychology

UNPREDICTABLE

//MATTHEW 10:38-39

"If you don't go all the way with me, through thick and thin, you don't deserve me. If your first concern is to look after yourself, you'll never find yourself. But if you forget about yourself and look to me, you'll find both yourself and me."

//REFLECT

Pulling up to the beach, I saw some homeless people. One of them looked like Rudolph, a man with whom I'd become friends a few months before. He was a middle-aged black man who was dying from Hepatitis C. When I pulled up, I knew Rudolph had not seen me, so I ignored God's voice telling me to go talk to him. *If God wants me to talk to Rudolph, He'll keep him there until I get back to the car*, I told myself. And that's just what God did. Hesitantly, I went over to Rudolph. As always, Rudolph was excited to see me. He introduced me to his friends,

PRAYER & SOLITUDE

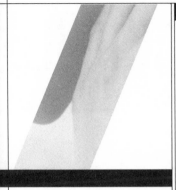

and then he instructed me to preach to them. I didn't want to go over and talk to Rudolph because it was inconvenient for me. I was looking after only myself. But when I obeyed God, He blessed me with the opportunity to share Jesus with people who wanted to listen. If I hadn't forgotten about myself, I would have missed God's purpose for me in that moment.

//PRAY

Oh, God, the more I feel Your call to do something for You, the more ashamed I feel for all I don't do. When did commitment to Christ become optional? Why don't I act when You tell me to? Why aren't my convictions strong enough to make me act? What's holding me back?

Maybe I'm the only one who wrestles with these questions, but I doubt it. Today, get alone with God and discuss these questions with Him. Ask Him to change your heart and to make you more sensitive to the people He wants to touch through you. Pray for forgiveness for the times He told you to do something and you disobeyed. Also ask Him to protect you from being overtaken by pride in those times when you do act and He uses you. Finally, ask God to set you free from worrying about what other people may think about you. Ask Him to make you more afraid of disobeying the Holy Spirit than what others may say about you.

Dennis Marinello
Age: 19
Major: undeclared

UNPREDICTABLE

ACTION

// MARK 1:16-20

Passing along the beach of Lake Galilee, he saw Simon and his brother Andrew net-fishing. Fishing was their regular work. Jesus said to them, "Come with me. I'll make a new kind of fisherman out of you. I'll show you how to catch men and women instead of perch and bass." They didn't ask questions. They dropped their nets and followed.

A dozen yards or so down the beach, he saw the brothers James and John, Zebedee's sons. They were in the boat, mending their fishnets. Right off, he made the same offer. Immediately, they left their father Zebedee, the boat, and the hired hands, and followed.

//REFLECT

I try every day not to judge others based on what I hear about them or how they dress, but it is really hard. I look at people who are different from me and slap labels on them. When I see people dressed either goth or emo, I label them as "attention fishers" or "freaks" in my head. Just today I saw this guy on a trolley system between our school's campuses. He had on this strange hat and these pants with all kinds of weird stuff stitched on them. To me, his clothes screamed out for attention, and that's how I labeled him. I know it was wrong, but I made up my mind right then that I did not want to become friends with him. I didn't even speak to him, all because of the clothes he was wearing.

//ACT

Jesus didn't condemn and reject people because of how they looked or what they had done. Genesis 1:27 says every person is created in the image of God, and that's how Jesus treated everyone He met. Today, when you see someone you would normally judge, remind yourself that the guy wearing the strange hat and funky pants reflects God's nature. And at least once today, begin a conversation with one of those people. Don't think of anyone as ordinary. Instead, look at every human being God brings across your path as a unique individual made in His image. How will this change the way you treat others? How does this change the way you think of sinful and destructive behavior in others? What kind of potential lies inside people you would normally dismiss? Perhaps this is why Jesus chose people no one else would ever think of using. He looked beyond the surface and saw possibilities, not problems.

Garrett Lowe
Age: 20
Majors: business; premed

UNPREDICTABLE

//MY FOCUS: MATTHEW 24:37-42

"The Arrival of the Son of Man will take place in times like Noah's. Before the great flood everyone was carrying on as usual, having a good time right up to the day Noah boarded the ark. They knew nothing—until the flood hit and swept everything away.

"The Son of Man's Arrival will be like that: Two men will be working in the field—one will be taken, one left behind; two women will be grinding at the mill—one will be taken, one left behind. So stay awake, alert. You have no idea what day your Master will show up."

//MY GOD

There was a time when I was really on fire for God. Then in my senior year of high school, it all fell apart. I became bitter, stressed, fed up, and out of patience for life. The change came about, by and large, due to a bad relationship I was in. After it ended, I gave up spiritually. Then, when I turned twenty-one, I started drinking. Even though I only got drunk twice, I started responding to every problem by saying, "I need a drink." It is amazing what we *think* we need.

As difficult as it is to maintain a healthy relationship with God, it is much harder to rebuild it. Scaling the "steps of righteousness" is far more difficult a second time.

MY JOURNEY

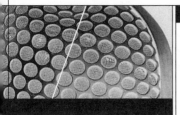

//MY PRAYER

I pray that I will give up this foolishness and make a final stand for Christ. I ask God for guidance and help in this and look to Him to lead me. I confess that I am weak and pathetic, crumbling under the pressures of life with little resistance. I cannot do anything without God's help. As Psalm 62:1 says,

> God, the one and only—
>   I'll wait as long as he says.
> Everything I need comes from
>   him.

This is my prayer.

There are fewer footholds than when you first climbed. After a while, I stopped trying. Now I live in a paradox. I want to be a wholehearted follower of Christ, but it is so difficult that I just do not want to try anymore. I hate feeling this way. I hate where I am in my walk, which only makes things harder. I'm continually reminded of how much I have regressed.

//MY THOUGHTS

Eventually I need to face reality. I need to address the pain, anger, and stress that are in my life. Substances can never take the place of God's healing hand. I need to break down completely, fall at the cross, and cry out, "I'm through! Lord, take me! I cannot stand to hide from You any longer. I'm Yours, Lord. Take me as You will."

Joseph A. Ellis IV
Age: 21
Major: psychology

//JOURNALING: LUKE 9:12-14

As the day declined, the Twelve said, "Dismiss the crowd so they can go to the farms or villages around here and get a room for the night and a bite to eat. We're out in the middle of nowhere."

"You feed them," Jesus said.

They said, "We couldn't scrape up more than five loaves of bread and a couple of fish—unless, of course, you want us to go to town ourselves and buy food for everybody." (There were more than five thousand people in the crowd.)

Jesus doesn't just do the unpredictable. He asks us to join Him in it. Look back over the week. What keeps you from joining Him? What surprises has He pulled on you over the past month? What does it mean to follow a Savior you can't completely figure out?

DAY

1

2

3

4

5

6

7

OBEDIENT

//MATTHEW 26:36-46

Then Jesus went with them to a garden called Gethsemane and told his disciples, "Stay here while I go over there and pray." Taking along Peter and the two sons of Zebedee, he plunged into an agonizing sorrow. Then he said, "This sorrow is crushing my life out. Stay here and keep vigil with me."

Going a little ahead, he fell on his face, praying, "My Father, if there is any way, get me out of this. But please, not what I want. You, what do *you* want?"

When he came back to his disciples, he found them sound asleep. He said to Peter, "Can't you stick it out with me a single hour? Stay alert; be in prayer so you don't wander into temptation without even knowing you're in danger. There is a part of you that is eager, ready for anything in God. But there's another part that's as lazy as an old dog sleeping by the fire."

He then left them a second time. Again he prayed, "My Father, if there is no other way than this, drinking this cup to the dregs, I'm ready. Do it your way."

When he came back, he again found them sound asleep. They simply couldn't keep their eyes open. This time he let them sleep on, and went back a third time to pray, going over the same ground one last time.

When he came back the next time, he said, "Are you going to

BIBLE READING

sleep on and make a night of it? My time is up, the Son of Man is about to be handed over to the hands of sinners. Get up! Let's get going! My betrayer is here."

//REFLECT

The Christian confession of faith consists of three little words: Jesus is Lord. These words mean Jesus rules our lives because He rules over the created universe. He is Lord of all. He makes the rules. He tells people what to do. He speaks, and others scramble to do what He says. Yet one of the defining characteristics of Jesus was His obedience to others. He obeyed His earthly parents, and He obeyed His heavenly Father. In fact, He said He never did anything on His own. All His acts came in response to directions from the Father through the Holy Spirit. This week you will be challenged to imitate Jesus' divine humility by obeying the authorities God has placed over your life.

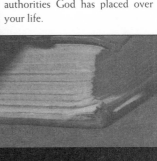

OBEDIENT

ACTION

//LUKE 2:41-51

Every year Jesus' parents traveled to Jerusalem for the Feast of Passover. When he was twelve years old, they went up as they always did for the Feast. When it was over and they left for home, the child Jesus stayed behind in Jerusalem, but his parents didn't know it. Thinking he was somewhere in the company of pilgrims, they journeyed for a whole day and then began looking for him among relatives and neighbors. When they didn't find him, they went back to Jerusalem looking for him.

The next day they found him in the Temple seated among the teachers, listening to them and asking questions. The teachers were all quite taken with him, impressed with the sharpness of his answers. But his parents were not impressed; they were upset and hurt.

His mother said, "Young man, why have you done this to us? Your father and I have been half out of our minds looking for you."

He said, "Why were you looking for me? Didn't you know that I had to be here, dealing with the things of my Father?" But they had no idea what he was talking about.

So he went back to Nazareth with them, and lived obediently with them.

//REFLECT

Growing up, I regularly found myself in situations in which my agenda conflicted with my parents' plans. Rather than just do as I was told, I fought for what I wanted. Even simple things such as taking out the trash became flash points. It wasn't that I wanted to do anything bad. I just wanted to set my own agenda. Jesus' example in today's passage shows how wrong I was. If Jesus obeyed His parents and those in authority over Him even though He is Lord of the universe, how much more so should I?

//ACT

Make a commitment to submit to the will of your parents and those in authority around you. Today, do at least one task that shows obedience to your parents (of course, you can do more if you want!). Whether you take out the trash, wash the dishes, or take care of your little brother or sister so your parents can take a break, find something you can do to help them. By doing so you will show them that you appreciate their impact on your life. Think about Jesus' reaction when His parents found Him in the Temple. He didn't whine or get angry. Instead, He showed kindness and obedience. Follow His example this week.

Andrew Porter
Age: 21
Major: youth ministry

OBEDIENT

//JOHN 5:19-20

So Jesus explained himself at length. "I'm telling you this straight. The Son can't independently do a thing, only what he sees the Father doing. What the Father does, the Son does. The Father loves the Son and includes him in everything he is doing."

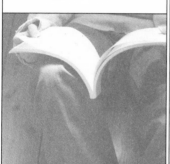

//REFLECT

Who are you listening to in your life? Friends, parents, coaches, teachers . . . God? To find out, take a pen and paper to a quiet spot in your house or outside. Make a list of all the things you do in a typical week. Include all your general activities, such as sleeping, eating, soccer practice, class, youth group, and so on. Put all those on the left side of your paper. In the middle of the paper, write down why you do these activities. Finally, on the right side, write down who you

PRAYER & SOLITUDE

//PRAY

Jesus lived His entire life to fulfill His Father's purposes. He had one goal: pleasing God. Pray and beg God for a heart like Jesus'. It is so easy to get caught up in the distractions of life that before you know it, God's plans get lost in the shuffle. Pray for wisdom to see the things on your list that need to be eliminated. Ask God what needs to be added to the list to obey His purpose for your life. Pray that you can glorify God through everything you do. Take these seven minutes of solitude to ask God to take charge of your life.

Peter Sherman
Age: 21
Major: youth ministry

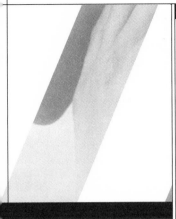

are doing these actions for. This list can include multiple people for each activity: yourself, your parents, a coach, and so forth. As you look over your list, ask yourself, *How much of God's plan for my life is reflected in what I actually do each day?*

OBEDIENT

"I came down from heaven not to follow my own whim but to accomplish the will of the One who sent me."

//REFLECT

Many times in our daily lives we make lists of things we need to accomplish throughout the day: "Pick up this," "Drop off that," and "Go there at 3:00 p.m." rule our lives. Looking back on our day, it can be hard to even remember what we said and to whom we said it. And it's on days like these that we forget about who we are and what our lives should count for. We forget that we were put on earth by God for a purpose. The purpose God has for His people is not to make hourly deadlines or fill empty spaces. The purpose is to do His will. His will is that we love Him and those around us in all we do. Jesus is the perfect example of this because He kept His mind on what God's will was for Him. Jesus knew that the time He was given was to be used to accomplish God's purposes.

FASTING

//THE NEXT LEVEL

- What did you learn from letting go of your planner?
- Did you discover activities you normally do that waste time? Were there activities that are selfish and not lined up with God's will?
- What did you learn in your time of sitting and listening to God?
- Did you hear God speak? What did He say about His will for your life?

Nicholas Thorn-Sermeno
Age: 22
Major: biblical studies

Courtney Bacon
Age: 21
Major: Christian ministries

//FAST

For the remainder of this week, take a fast from schedules. Although you still need to keep important obligations such as going to class or work, put your calendar down and fast from planning every minute of your day. Take time to do nothing but sit and listen to God. Set aside twenty minutes or two hours, whatever works for you, to sit in silence before God. Spend the time you would normally spend running around and give it to God to use however He wants.

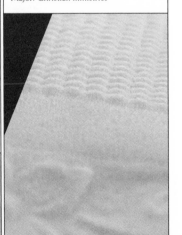

OBEDIENT

JOHN 14:28

"The Father is the goal and purpose of my life."

LUKE 10:38-42

As they continued their travel, Jesus entered a village. A woman by the name of Martha welcomed him and made him feel quite at home. She had a sister, Mary, who sat before the Master, hanging on every word he said. But Martha was pulled away by all she had to do in the kitchen. Later, she stepped in, interrupting them. "Master, don't you care that my sister has abandoned the kitchen to me? Tell her to lend me a hand."

The Master said, "Martha, dear Martha, you're fussing far too much and getting yourself worked up over nothing. One thing only is essential, and Mary has chosen it—it's the main course, and won't be taken from her."

MY JOURNEY

//MY GOD

I want my entire life to have but one purpose: to follow God. He calls me to imitate Christ and make Him the goal and purpose of my life. But I find it is so easy to claim that I'm living for God just because my day planner is filled with things I do for Him. And even though doing things for Jesus is a good thing, it must be blanketed by true obedience. Jesus told Martha in Luke 10:42 that "one thing only is essential." That *one thing* is knowing the Father. We can busy ourselves doing good things for God and still not fulfill His purpose for our lives. Being obedient to God means making Him the goal of our lives instead of focusing on what we do for Him. I wonder what would happen if I spent more time with God and less time doing things for Him.

//MY PRAYER

My prayer is for me to *stop!* Stop with my busy life, even if it is filled with doing good deeds. And start filling my time with moments spent with God. I pray that God, not the things I do for Him, would become the goal and purpose of my life.

//MY THOUGHTS

- Am I spending so much time thinking of what I can *do* for God that I never spend any time with Him?
- Without Christ, all is in vain. What have I done today in vain?
- If I busy myself with things of God but don't make Him a part of them, what's the point?

Liz Wade
Age: 21
Major: youth ministry

OBEDIENT

From there Jesus set out for the vicinity of Tyre. He entered a house there where he didn't think he would be found, but he couldn't escape notice. He was barely inside when a woman who had a disturbed daughter heard where he was. She came and knelt at his feet, begging for help. The woman was Greek, Syro-Phoenician by birth. She asked him to cure her daughter.

He said, "Stand in line and take your turn. The children get fed first. If there's any left over, the dogs get it."

She said, "Of course, Master. But don't dogs under the table get scraps dropped by the children?"

Jesus was impressed. "You're right! On your way! Your daughter is no longer disturbed. The demonic affliction is gone."

PRAISE &
CELEBRATION

//PRAISE

Have you ever thought about your body language when you come before God? For me, I find that words are not always enough. The simple act of kneeling in recognition of how truly awesome our Lord is can sometimes be all the language I need to connect with God. Today, I challenge you to think about your body language while you praise and worship Him. Maybe it is raising your hands, maybe it is bowing your head, or maybe it is lying down. Whatever it may be, speak to God today with both your words and your body. Physically show Him how you feel inside.

//PRAY

God, may I continue to fall to my knees and recognize that You are Lord. I cannot do this on my own. I ask that You will show me Your ways. I ask that You will speak to me through Your people, through Your creation, and through the silence. May my open hands be a symbol of surrender to You, God. Fill me with Your Holy Spirit so that I may be obedient to Your purpose and will for my life. Thank You for Your love and grace.

Janelle Comfort
Age: 20
Major: youth ministry

//JOURNALING: MARK 1:9-13

At this time, Jesus came from Nazareth in Galilee and was baptized by John in the Jordan. The moment he came out of the water, he saw the sky split open and God's Spirit, looking like a dove, come down on him. Along with the Spirit, a voice: "You are my Son, chosen and marked by my love, pride of my life."

At once, this same Spirit pushed Jesus out into the wild. For forty wilderness days and nights he was tested by Satan. Wild animals were his companions, and angels took care of him.

Obeying God doesn't mean our lives will be one happy event after another. But then, why would we think it should? What do you need to do to start obeying God? What stands in your way?

HOLY

Next Jesus was taken into the wild by the Spirit for the Test. The Devil was ready to give it. Jesus prepared for the Test by fasting forty days and forty nights. That left him, of course, in a state of extreme hunger, which the Devil took advantage of in the first test: "Since you are God's Son, speak the word that will turn these stones into loaves of bread."

Jesus answered by quoting Deuteronomy: "It takes more than bread to stay alive. It takes a steady stream of words from God's mouth."

For the second test the Devil took him to the Holy City. He sat him on top of the Temple and said, "Since you are God's Son, jump." The Devil goaded him by quoting Psalm 91: "He

has placed you in the care of angels. They will catch you so that you won't so much as stub your toe on a stone."

Jesus countered with another citation from Deuteronomy: "Don't you dare test the Lord your God."

For the third test, the Devil took him on the peak of a huge mountain. He gestured expansively, pointing out all the earth's kingdoms, how glorious they all were. Then he said, "They're yours—lock, stock, and barrel. Just go down on your knees and worship me, and they're yours."

Jesus' refusal was curt: "Beat it, Satan!" He backed his rebuke with a third quotation from Deuteronomy: "Worship the

BIBLE READING

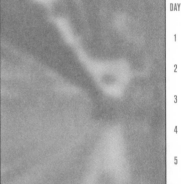

Lord your God, and only him. Serve him with absolute single-heartedness."

The Test was over. The Devil left. And in his place, angels! Angels came and took care of Jesus' needs.

//REFLECT

Jesus lived a holy life even when faced with a constant barrage of temptation. That's the theme for this week. We will explore Jesus' holiness in the real world, not as a cold doctrine removed from the day-to-day realities of life. His holiness was put to the ultimate test and proved to be real. Will yours?

HOLY

ACTION

//1 PETER 1:13-16

So roll up your sleeves, put your mind in gear, be totally ready to receive the gift that's coming when Jesus arrives. Don't lazily slip back into those old grooves of evil, doing just what you feel like doing. You didn't know any better then; you do now. As obedient children, let yourselves be pulled into a way of life shaped by God's life, a life energetic and blazing with holiness. God said, "I am holy; you be holy."

//REFLECT

As followers of Christ, we have only two options when it comes to holiness. Either we embrace God's call fully, or we remain attached to our own desires. Holiness is not something we can do halfway. Obedience in only one area of our lives falls short of meeting God's standards, for He says to be holy in everything.

//ACT

When we strive to live holy lives, the lure to go back to our sinful ways often seems stronger than it was before. Therefore, it is absolutely essential that you let God change you from the inside out with His Word. When Jesus was tempted in the wilderness, He responded to Satan by quoting Scripture. But Jesus didn't just know the Word; He lived it. Allow God to shape you in the same way by making a commitment to set apart time this week (and beyond) to read the Bible. This practice will not only help you know how to respond to temptation, but it will also strengthen your heart and mind. Start with the story of Jesus Himself, the best example of a holy life. Begin with Matthew and work your way through the Gospels, spending thirty minutes every day. The results will exceed your expectations. Your actions will radiate with the holiness that is in your heart.

//THE NEXT LEVEL

Getting yourself into a routine of reading the Bible every day is a great accomplishment, but maintaining the habit is an even greater challenge. That is why you need to stay active in the Word. Don't let your interaction with the Bible stop at merely reading it. Memorize encouraging verses once a month, set apart time for meditation on a convicting passage every week, and remain faithful to prayer before, during, and after every reading, balancing requests and praises. Let yourself be pulled into Scripture. Let your life be shaped by it, for it is God's Word to us.

Rachel Pietka
Age: 21
Major: English with a concentration in literature

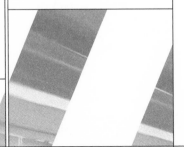

HOLY

//MATTHEW 18:8-9

"If your hand or your foot gets in the way of God, chop it off and throw it away. You're better off maimed or lame and alive than the proud owners of two hands and two feet, godless in a furnace of eternal fire. And if your eye distracts you from God, pull it out and throw it away. You're better off one-eyed and alive than exercising your twenty-twenty vision from inside the fire of hell."

//REFLECT

God wants us to have a relationship with Him, and He doesn't want anything to stand in the way. That's what this passage is saying. We need to get rid of anything that keeps us away from God. This is where fasting comes in. Fasting shows us how fragile and fickle we are, and at the same time, it soothes us with God's love. It gives us time to reflect on our lives and priorities. True fasting is more than a rejection of food or the world, but a search for holiness—a search in which we must pass beyond the stage of preferring something else to God. As Jesus said, "Seek first the kingdom of God."

Everything in this world separates us from God. For us as students, it can be papers, deadlines, lack of time, or tests. Our hectic schedules cause us to drift away from Him. When we fast, we are reminded how much we must rely upon God to survive. More than that, we're pulled back into the relationship God seeks with us.

FASTING

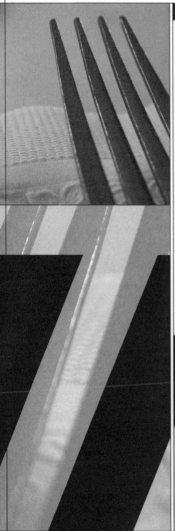

//FAST

Today's fast is a traditional fast from food. How long you should go without eating is difficult to pinpoint, but perhaps try a twenty-four-hour period. The fast should last long enough for you to engage in meaningful prayer and reflection. This isn't just about going without food. Instead, the fast shows your desire to seek more of God. While fasting, avoid carbonated drinks. Your stomach will appreciate it. Instead, drink water or fruit juices. Above all, spend the time in prayer. Let your stomach's growls remind you of your soul's hunger for God and His holiness.

Nadia Ramirez
Age: 23
Major: international business

HOLY

//2 CORINTHIANS 5:20-21

We're Christ's representatives. God uses us to persuade men and women to drop their differences and enter into God's work of making things right between them. We're speaking for Christ himself now: Become friends with God; he's already a friend with you.

How? you say. In Christ. God put the wrong on him who never did anything wrong, so we could be put right with God.

//REFLECT

Do you ever have a day when you feel as if you cannot do a single thing you know God wants you to do? God tells me to be patient, yet I become infuriated by the morning traffic. God tells me to treat others the way I would want to be treated, yet I still secretly criticize the outfit of the girl next to me. I try to justify my actions by saying that no one is getting hurt, but I know better. Sure, I may not always intend to screw up, but that doesn't make me any less sinful. There are so many moments in every day when I subconsciously—and consciously—sin.

PRAYER & SOLITUDE

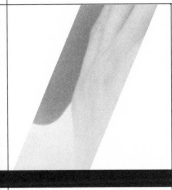

Here's the scary part: These verses say I am Christ's representative. I don't know how that makes you feel, but for me, to represent a perfect, sinless, holy Person the way that I do is—well, let's just say it's a little misleading. In Christ I am a saint, but I am still a sinful person, and Lord knows (and He really does) that I can never be perfect. But thankfully for me, that's not the end of the story. The one Person in the world who never did anything wrong gets the rap for every wrong thing that everyone else has ever done. Good thing I'm not the Messiah because there's no way I'm taking the punishment for something I didn't do. But Jesus did. And now I'm supposed to represent Him to the world.

//PRAY

Go to a quiet place where you can really focus on God. Before you start to pray, close your eyes and, with your palms down, clench your fists for fifteen to thirty seconds. As you release, turn your hands over and exhale. Start your prayer by letting go of all the worries and stresses of the day. Then really focus on what keeps you from being a holy representative of Jesus. Ask God for forgiveness and then ask Him for help in those areas. End your prayer by thanking God for sending His holy Son to take the blame for our sins.

Sarah Day
Age: 21
Major: natural science

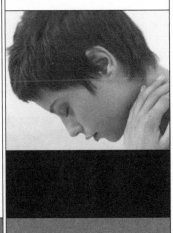

HOLY

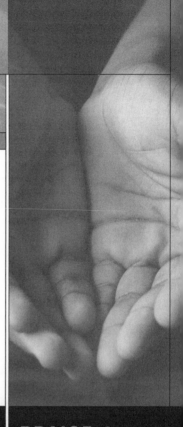

//1 PETER 1:5-7

God is keeping careful watch over us and the future. The Day is coming when you'll have it all—life healed and whole.

I know how great this makes you feel, even though you have to put up with every kind of aggravation in the meantime. Pure gold put in the fire comes out of it *proved* pure; genuine faith put through this suffering comes out *proved* genuine. When Jesus wraps this all up, it's your faith, not your gold, that God will have on display as evidence of his victory.

PRAISE & CELEBRATION

//REFLECT

Ninety-nine percent pure gold does not just pop out of the ground in perfect blocks. Miners dig out ore in which gold is intermixed with all kinds of metals and minerals. They pulverize the ore to get to the gold. Ultimately, the mix goes into a fire where all the impurities can be removed. Then and only then can the gold be used to make jewelry and all the other stuff it is used for today.

Our faith must go through the fire just like gold. God doesn't just drop holiness down on us from out of the sky. He uses trials and suffering as His refiner's fire. The process doesn't feel very good, but there is no other way. To God, our faith is worth far more than the finest gold the world has ever seen, and He is willing to do whatever it takes to make it pure.

//PRAISE

Make a list of all the trials and suffering you've faced lately. How has God used them to refine your faith? You may not be able to answer that question yet. Too often we allow difficult times to make us angry with God, and we don't let Him use them to change us. Today, look at the circumstances God has taken you through lately from His perspective. Praise Him for loving you enough to refine your faith and your character. Thank Him for making you holy through the fire of trials.

HOLY

//MY FOCUS: HEBREWS 12:2-4

Keep your eyes on *Jesus*, who both began and finished this race we're in. Study how he did it. Because he never lost sight of where he was headed—that exhilarating finish in and with God—he could put up with anything along the way: cross, shame, whatever. And now he's *there*, in the place of honor, right alongside God. When you find yourselves flagging in your faith, go over that story again, item by item, that long litany of hostility he plowed through. *That* will shoot adrenaline into your souls!

In this all-out match against sin, others have suffered far worse than you, to say nothing of what Jesus went through—all that bloodshed!

MY JOURNEY

//MY GOD

Each day, sin shows up in my life. It causes me to lose my focus and fall away from the path I want to stay on. But even though I sin, Jesus Christ offers Himself as the perfect sacrifice and the perfect example. He never loses sight of God, regardless of the obstacles He has faced. So often I say I long to be like Jesus, but I lack initiative because of the sin that keeps tripping me up. But why should that stop me?

Jesus endured so much, and it is for this reason that He understands my struggles. He dealt with the pain and the shame and suffered more than I could possibly know. His eyes were fixed on that finish line, and with God as His focus, how could He not finish strong? Jesus became the model for me, and now it is my turn to run to Him. Jesus suffered so that I might be set apart for God. Now I have to respond.

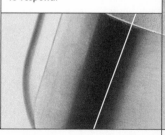

//MY THOUGHTS

- What can I do today to help me focus more on God?
- What sins in my life are causing me to lose sight of God?
- How will I deal with the next obstacle that could potentially cause me to lose my focus?

Dustin Reynolds
Age: 20
Major: biblical studies

//MY PRAYER

Lord God, I know that so often I lose my focus. I pray that each day You will become clearer and clearer to me as I strive to be like You. Help me to identify those areas of my life that are stopping me from being closer to You. I pray that the next time life gets hard, I will be reminded of the perseverance and strength You showed throughout Your life. Thank You, Lord, for what You did for me on the cross, taking on my sin so that I might become holy through You.

//JOURNALING: TITUS 2:11-14

God's readiness to give and forgive is now public. Salvation's available for everyone! We're being shown how to turn our backs on a godless, indulgent life, and how to take on a God-filled, God-honoring life. This new life is starting right now, and is whetting our appetites for the glorious day when our great God and Savior, Jesus Christ, appears. He offered himself as a sacrifice to free us from a dark, rebellious life into this good, pure life, making us a people he can be proud of, energetic in goodness.

Holiness doesn't mean keeping rules. Instead, it means allowing God to transform every aspect of our lives as part of our relationship with Him. After exploring holiness this week, how are you doing? Where do you struggle? How is God working in your life to make His holiness a reality in you?

SACRIFICE

When Jesus arrived in the villages of Caesarea Philippi, he asked his disciples, "What are people saying about who the Son of Man is?"

They replied, "Some think he is John the Baptizer, some say Elijah, some Jeremiah or one of the other prophets."

He pressed them, "And how about you? Who do you say I am?"

Simon Peter said, "You're the Christ, the Messiah, the Son of the living God."

Jesus came back, "God bless you, Simon, son of Jonah! You didn't get that answer out of books or from teachers. My Father in heaven, God himself, let you in on this secret of who

I really am. And now I'm going to tell you who you are, *really* are. You are Peter, a rock. This is the rock on which I will put together my church, a church so expansive with energy that not even the gates of hell will be able to keep it out.

"And that's not all. You will have complete and free access to God's kingdom, keys to open any and every door: no more barriers between heaven and earth, earth and heaven. A yes on earth is yes in heaven. A no on earth is no in heaven."

He swore the disciples to secrecy. He made them promise they would tell no one that he was the Messiah.

Then Jesus made it clear to his disciples that it was now

BIBLE READING

necessary for him to go to Jerusalem, submit to an ordeal of suffering at the hands of the religious leaders, be killed, and then on the third day be raised up alive.

//REFLECT

Once the disciples finally figured out that Jesus really was the Messiah, the chosen One from God, He began telling them about how He would be put to death and be raised up on the third day. The fact that it took them so long to understand all He had been telling them about who He was explains why they didn't understand it when He told them what He had to do. Jesus came to earth to die on a cross. He came to offer Himself as the final sacrifice for the sins of the world. Christ died so that we would no longer live for ourselves but for Him. We are now to imitate His sacrifice by giving ourselves to Him and to others.

SACRIFICE

//MARK 15:16-20

The soldiers took Jesus into the palace (called Praetorium) and called together the entire brigade. They dressed him up in purple and put a crown plaited from a thorn bush on his head. Then they began their mockery: "Bravo, King of the Jews!" They banged on his head with a club, spit on him, and knelt down in mock worship. After they had had their fun, they took off the purple cape and put his own clothes back on him. Then they marched out to nail him to the cross.

//REFLECT

To learn more about Jesus' sacrifice, read Mark 15:1-47. Imagine that you are part of that large crowd, slowly making your way up to Golgotha. You are not sure if you are being pushed along by the crowd or pulled along by a force you cannot explain. You reach the top of the hill, and the crowd stops. Your eyes rest on three crosses that lie on the ground. Soon the pounding of steel resonates all around you as soldiers start to nail the prisoners to each cross. You watch as the crosses are slowly raised into the air, one by one. The air is filled

PRAYER & SOLITUDE

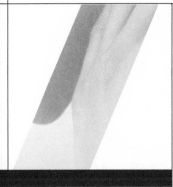

//PRAY

Allow yourself to kneel there at the foot of the cross and reflect upon what this means for you. And pray, *Thank You, God, that You became human to save us. You took the punishment upon Yourself and gave away Your life for the same people who have rejected and deceived You, who have made Your death necessary, and who have refused to believe.*

Tamra Danenhauer
Age: 21
Major: communications

with the sound of skin ripping and pain-filled cries from the prisoners. Your eyes are especially drawn to the One in the middle. You've heard of this Man before. He is the One who calls Himself "King of the Jews." He sure doesn't look like a king now, blood pouring down His face, His body wracked with pain. But as you continue to look at Him, you notice His eyes. They seem to look right through to your soul. They seem to be saying, "I'm doing this for you."

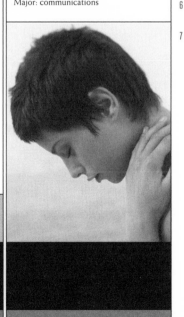

SACRIFICE

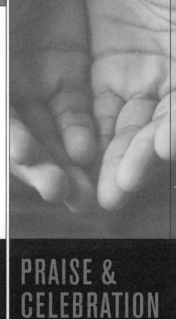

//1 JOHN 4:9-11

This is how God showed his love for us: God sent his only Son into the world so we might live through him. This is the kind of love we are talking about—not that we once upon a time loved God, but that he loved us and sent his Son as a sacrifice to clear away our sins and the damage they've done to our relationship with God.

My dear, dear friends, if God loved us like this, we certainly ought to love each other.

PRAISE & CELEBRATION

//REFLECT

Sometimes I live like I don't care about the price God paid for my sins. I'm too busy trying to follow my own path. I desecrate Jesus' cross through my selfish actions. When I think about what Jesus did on the cross, I should cringe in shame because of my sin. Jesus the King was mocked, spat on, beaten, whipped, and crucified despite the fact that He knew we would turn our backs on Him someday. God could have justifiably separated us from Him for eternity, but because of His unconditional love, He made a way for us to be set right with Him.

//PRAISE

We can't afford to lose track of Christ's love for us; if we do, our faith and our walk are vulnerable to our own devices, our own weaknesses that make us feel like we are God. Today, set your eyes on Christ's sacrifice and write Him a letter of thanks. Don't rush through this or write down a bunch of Sunday school phrases. Think about where you would be without His sacrifice, both now and forever. Then take an honest look at your life and how you live in light of Jesus' dying for you. Remember as well how all this started. God loved us first. Now, in this letter, love Him back. Tell Him what's in your heart as you think about everything He did for you. After you finish writing the letter, read it out loud to God as an act of worship. After you finish, put it in a safe place. Pull it out and read it again at least once today before you go to bed and again before the week is over. Feel free to add something new each time you read it.

Joy Collins
Age: 20
Major: cinema broadcast arts

SACRIFICE

ACTION

//2 CORINTHIANS 5:14-18

Christ's love has moved me to such extremes. His love has the first and last word in everything we do.

Our firm decision is to work from this focused center: One man died for everyone. That puts everyone in the same boat. He included everyone in his death so that everyone could also be included in his life, a resurrection life, a far better life than people ever lived on their own.

Because of this decision we don't evaluate people by what they have or how they look. We looked at the Messiah that way once and got it all wrong, as you know. We certainly don't look at him that way anymore. Now we look inside, and what we see is that anyone united with the Messiah gets a fresh start, is created new. The old life is gone; a new life burgeons! Look at it! All this comes from the God who settled the relationship between us and him, and then called us to settle our relationships with each other.

//REFLECT

God gives us this amazing chance to make everything new in our relationship with Him, but He doesn't want to stop there. Once He settles His relationship with us, He calls us to smooth out conflicts with each other. Doing this means we have to swallow our pride and sacrifice the appearance of having it all together to make things right with those we may have hurt. This sounds hard until we look at the cross of Christ. Jesus sacrificed His reputation and His life to build relationships with those who seemed undeserving. Shouldn't we do the same?

//ACT

I challenge you to change one relationship in your life that isn't whole. Sacrifice your pride and humbly ask that person for forgiveness. If someone has acted standoffish to you, ask her why and apologize for anything you might have done to cause her to act that way. As you begin doing this one relationship at a time, you will do what Jesus calls each of His children to do. Your life will begin to be transformed, and you will begin to view your relationships with others as the second most important focus in your life, second only to your relationship with God.

Ilise Lauman
Age: 19
Major: communications

SACRIFICE

//ROMANS 14:8-9

It's *God* we are answerable to—all the way from life to death and everything in between—not each other. That's why Jesus lived and died and then lived again: so that he could be our Master across the entire range of life and death, and free us from the petty tyrannies of each other.

//REFLECT

Think for a moment about what you are wearing today. How long did it take you to choose the outfit and then actually get ready? I admit that when planning my day, I take into consideration how long it will take me to get dressed, change my outfit at least two times, put on my makeup, style my hair, and then accessorize. (Guys, you can relate when you wonder which hat to throw on or which underwear is clean.) When you look at it like this, it's obvious that we are overly concerned with our image—and clothes are just the beginning of it! *Enough is enough!*

FASTING

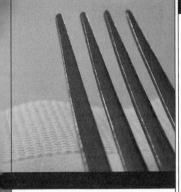

//FAST

Today, fast from dodging criticism by making yourself vulnerable to it. Sacrifice your "polished" image. Don't wear any makeup. Wear old or generic clothes, laugh as loudly as you want, or eat onions on your burger. Maybe even humbly imitate a "flaw" that you often criticize in others. For instance, if you frequently mock others for wearing high waters, wear them yourself this week! Don't become defensive when people stare or laugh at you. Learn to be patient with others. Keep in mind that this is how others may feel when you judge and criticize them.

Renee Vaupel
Age: 20
Major: communications

Why are we so worried about "the petty tyrannies of each other" when we know that God is our Master and doesn't need to be impressed? Maybe we know that we consciously criticize others for their less-than-perfect images and fear that the same judgment will be turned around on us. God sent Christ to free us from criticism. We may not be perfect, but we are all seen as equally beautiful when covered in His redeeming blood. Our image is all the same in God's eyes, and this is truly how we're called to look at one another.

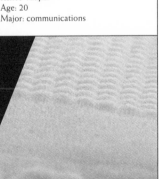

SACRIFICE

//MY FOCUS: ROMANS 3:23-25

//MY GOD

Since we've compiled this long and sorry record as sinners (both us and them) and proved that we are utterly incapable of living the glorious lives God wills for us, God did it for us. Out of sheer generosity he put us in right standing with himself. A pure gift. He got us out of the mess we're in and restored us to where he always wanted us to be. And he did it by means of Jesus Christ.

God sacrificed Jesus on the altar of the world to clear that world of sin. Having faith in him sets us in the clear. God decided on this course of action in full view of the public—to set the world in the clear with himself through the sacrifice of Jesus, finally taking care of the sins he had so patiently endured.

There are times when I try so hard to live the Christian life that I miss the point. I get so caught up in trying to figure out how to share my beliefs with others, make a difference in the world, become a better person, or find my purpose in life that I lose sight of why these even matter in the first place. Without Jesus' sacrifice, nothing else matters. Yet so often I find it easier to focus on these other peripheral issues instead. Why?

I think the answer may lie in the nature of Jesus' sacrifice. I can figure out peripheral issues, but I will never be able to comprehend why Jesus would die for me. Could my difficulty understanding Christ's sacrifice be a blessing in disguise? If I have something all figured out, I might assume

MY
JOURNEY

Heavenly Father, I don't understand You. It seems as if You do things in the most complicated way imaginable, but maybe that's the point. Please help me focus on You and Your incomprehensible sacrifice rather than on my problems and faults.

there's no need to think about it anymore. Why waste the time contemplating something I already understand? As long as I know that I don't understand something, I will keep going back to try to find new insights into previously unforeseen possibilities.

Christianity is not about *me* finding myself or having all the answers. It's about what *He* has already done, what He continues to do, and, more to the point, *why* He has done it. Unless we understand Him, how can we make sense of anything else?

Christopher Cazares
Age: 21
Majors: English; philosophy

//JOURNALING: GALATIANS 3:11-13

The obvious impossibility of carrying out such a moral program should make it plain that no one can sustain a relationship with God that way. The person who lives in right relationship with God does it by embracing what God arranges for him. Doing things for God is the opposite of entering into what God does for you. Habakkuk had it right: "The person who believes God, is set right by God—and that's the real life." Rule-keeping does not naturally evolve into living by faith, but only perpetuates itself in more and more rule-keeping, a fact observed in Scripture: "The one who does these things [rule-keeping] continues to live by them."

Christ redeemed us from that self-defeating, cursed life by absorbing it completely into himself. Do you remember the Scripture that says, "Cursed is everyone who hangs on a tree"? That is what happened when Jesus was nailed to the Cross: He became a curse, and at the same time dissolved the curse.

As you look back on this week, what thoughts crossed your mind as you contemplated Jesus' sacrifice for your sin?

DAY

1

2

3

4

5

6

7

ALIVE

// LUKE 24:1-12

At the crack of dawn on Sunday, the women came to the tomb carrying the burial spices they had prepared. They found the entrance stone rolled back from the tomb, so they walked in. But once inside, they couldn't find the body of the Master Jesus.

They were puzzled, wondering what to make of this. Then, out of nowhere it seemed, two men, light cascading over them, stood there. The women were awestruck and bowed down in worship. The men said, "Why are you looking for the Living One in a cemetery? He is not here, but raised up. Remember how he told you when you were still back in Galilee that he had to be handed over to sinners, be killed on a cross, and in three days rise up?" Then they remembered Jesus' words.

They left the tomb and broke the news of all this to the Eleven and the rest. Mary Magdalene, Joanna, Mary the mother of James, and the other women with them kept telling these things to the apostles, but the apostles didn't believe a word of it, thought they were making it all up.

But Peter jumped to his feet and ran to the tomb. He stooped to look in and saw a few grave clothes, that's all. He walked away puzzled, shaking his head.

BIBLE READING

//REFLECT

The angels' question is classic: "Why are you looking for the Living One in a cemetery?" Why would anyone look for the living Lord in the place of the dead? That doesn't make much sense. And that's the point. Our Savior isn't dead. He is alive, and our faith should be as well. The day Jesus walked out of the tomb, the disciples'—and our—lives changed forever. Since Jesus is really alive, how must we now live?

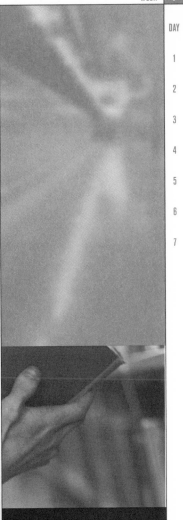

ALIVE

//ROMANS 6:11

From now on, think of it this way: Sin speaks a dead language that means nothing to you; God speaks your mother tongue, and you hang on every word. You are dead to sin and alive to God. That's what Jesus did.

//REFLECT

You know what's crazy about this passage? Most of the time it doesn't work out that way for me. Sin speaks a language I am very familiar with. And it speaks that language a whole lot louder than God speaks His. It's not that I don't understand what I hear from God; I'm just not always listening to Him. In fact, sometimes I specifically don't talk to Him about things because I don't want to hear what He has to say.

Listening to sin is easy. It promises quick fixes. And when will it tell me I'm in the wrong?

PRAYER & SOLITUDE

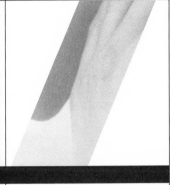

//SOLITUDE

Today, rather than talk to God, listen to Him. Get alone with Him in a quiet place and listen for His voice. Start off with the prayer Samuel prayed in 1 Samuel 3:10: "Speak. I'm your servant, ready to listen." Take your Bible with you and read it during this exercise. After all, it is God's Word. He speaks to us through it. Don't try to rush God. Listen for His voice. Then hang on to every word.

//PRAY

God, help me. I get stuck in the comfort of what I know. Please push me out of it. Open my ears to Your voice, even if what You have to say makes me uncomfortable. God, give me peace to trust that whatever You say and wherever You lead me will be better than where I am now. I want to hang on every word You say. I love You.

Christina Vickers
Age: 20
Major: communications

Never. I listen to sin, and nine times out of ten the whole world backs me up on it. But listening to God? That's another story. He tells me to do things I've never done before. He asks me to do things people around me just don't get. He has a high standard for me, and He won't stop until I reach it. He loves me too much to leave me where He found me.

That's scary stuff. I'm good with what I know. I can handle it. But listening to God takes me way out of my comfort zone. Listening to sin is a lot less risky (or so it seems), and sometimes that's enough to win me over.

ALIVE

ACTION

//1 JOHN 2:15-17

Don't love the world's ways. Don't love the world's goods. Love of the world squeezes out love for the Father. Practically everything that goes on in the world—wanting your own way, wanting everything for yourself, wanting to appear important—has nothing to do with the Father. It just isolates you from him. The world and all its wanting, wanting, wanting is on the way out—but whoever does what God wants is set for eternity.

//REFLECT

Jesus is alive, but this world is on the way out. That's why God calls Christians to stop loving what the world has to offer. Instead, we are to walk with the Lord. Walking alongside Jesus means laying aside selfishness and materialism. He leads us to love others just as He loves us. When we walk with Him, we will find gratification in meeting the needs of those around us. As we do, Jesus will come alive to us through the people we meet.

//ACT

Today, reflect on your human nature to be selfish, to want material things, and to desire fame. Every time you catch yourself being egocentric, give yourself a reality check. Think about others around you and figure out how you can be selfless and extend God's love to them. If you find yourself lusting after worldly possessions, remember those who are less fortunate than you.

To act on your reflections, go through your closet or even your entire room and look for things to offer those who have little. Don't confine this to possessions you no longer use or need. Make an actual sacrifice. In the name of the Lord, give someone something that is important to you.

Christopher Bunting
Age: 19
Major: communications

ALIVE

//COLOSSIANS 3:1-3

So if you're serious about living this new resurrection life with Christ, *act* like it. Pursue the things over which Christ presides. Don't shuffle along, eyes to the ground, absorbed with the things right in front of you. Look up, and be alert to what is going on around Christ—that's where the action is. See things from *his* perspective.

Your old life is dead. Your new life, which is your *real* life—even though invisible to spectators—is with Christ in God. *He* is your life.

FASTING

//REFLECT

Alive. What does it really mean to be alive? As I walk through the halls to class, am I really alive? As I go through the lines in the cafeteria, am I really alive? What is alive? I have a pulse; does that mean I am alive? I wonder if I have ever really lived. As I go through my days, I realize that I am not alive, but merely living. So many times I go through the motions and walk through the day just because I have to. I turn in the assignments and eat the food because I should. How much of my day do I spend *living*, and how much of it do I spend *alive*? I truly want to see the face of God in what I do, but when I look through gray eyes, where can He be found? I feel like my life is in black and white, and I want to see in color! I want to be alive! This is where this verse kicks in: "Your new life, which is your *real* life—even though invisible to spectators—is with Christ in God." When I look to the Lord, I start to see in color and really live.

//FAST

Today, fast from going through the motions. Stop seeing the world in black and white. Look for God's face in everything you do, asking Him to make you alive in every moment of the day. This isn't just some abstract idea. You can truly come alive, your world bursting with color. Don't go through the day just because you have to. Ask God to open up your eyes so you will see in color and feel His love.

Shannon Van Vorst
Age: 19
Major: communications

ALIVE

//EPHESIANS 2:1-6

It wasn't so long ago that you were mired in that old stagnant life of sin. You let the world, which doesn't know the first thing about living, tell you how to live. You filled your lungs with polluted unbelief, and then exhaled disobedience. We all did it, all of us doing what we felt like doing, when we felt like doing it, all of us in the same boat. It's a wonder God didn't lose his temper and do away with the whole lot of us. Instead, immense in mercy and with an incredible love, he embraced us. He took our sin-dead lives and made us alive in Christ. He did all this on his own, with no help from us! Then he picked us up and set us down in highest heaven in company with Jesus, our Messiah.

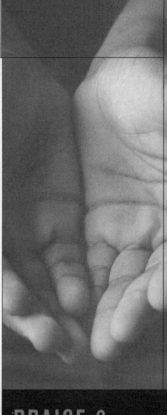

PRAISE & CELEBRATION

//REFLECT

When Jesus walked out of the tomb alive, He made us alive as well. Before coming to Christ, we were all dead in the "stagnant life of sin." Our hearts might have beat and air might have filled our lungs, but we were still dead. Spiritually, we were cut off from God, and that condition would have become permanent the moment our physical lives ran out. But God didn't leave us that way. He took our sin-dead lives and made us alive with Jesus. Previously, we existed on planet Earth. Now we live.

//PRAISE

If you were suddenly cured of a fatal disease, how would you spend your first healthy day? Whatever you would do is what I want you to do today as an act of praise to God. Don't take your life for granted. Don't waste all your time in front of a computer reading the latest postings on the Shins' website. You were dead, and God made you alive. Now what are you going to do? Show your gratitude to God by the way you use these next twenty-four hours.

ALIVE

//MY FOCUS: ROMANS 6:5-8

Each of us is raised into a light-filled world by our Father so that we can see where we're going in our new grace-sovereign country.

Could it be any clearer? Our old way of life was nailed to the Cross with Christ, a decisive end to that sin-miserable life—no longer at sin's every beck and call! What we believe is this: If we get included in Christ's sin-conquering death, we also get included in his life-saving resurrection.

//MY GOD

I'm tired of hoping that my life will have purpose. I'm fed up with trying to understand the concept that God has a plan for me. Why can't He give me some hint of what I should do with my life? I'm afraid I'll make a mistake that I will regret forever. I feel so lost right now. My life is passing me by, and I have lost control of the wheel. Every time I go to church or chapel and get on fire to live my life for Him, something goes wrong, and I mess up again. Sometimes I feel that my existence has no significant meaning. God tells me He has given me new life, but I just want to know why He has kept me alive when so many times I should have died.

MY JOURNEY

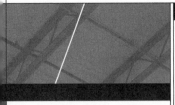

//MY PRAYER

I pray that I would continue to have faith in You and myself to make the right decisions in life. I long to live for You. I want to adjust my life to truly have faith and to live the Christian life. I pray that I will never wake up and find myself totally alone without You, Lord.

Yvania A. Garcia
Age: 20
Majors: journalism; political science

I know that He has a plan for everyone; it's just a matter of finding out what it is. This road of life is very scary, and I have come to realize that I am never really alone. Even in my frustration He stays right next to me, walking down the path of life. He will be there to catch me when I fall and to pick me up when it seems I can't go on. I'm afraid I will fail in life and fail Him. I know that I must forget about the world and just follow Him. I know that if I continue to have faith in Him, He will lead me down the path of righteousness.

//JOURNALING: 1 CORINTHIANS 15:16-20

If corpses can't be raised, then Christ wasn't, because he was indeed dead. And if Christ weren't raised, then all you're doing is wandering about in the dark, as lost as ever. It's even worse for those who died hoping in Christ and resurrection, because they're already in their graves. If all we get out of Christ is a little inspiration for a few short years, we're a pretty sorry lot. But the truth is that Christ *has* been raised up, the first in a long legacy of those who are going to leave the cemeteries.

The Christian life isn't about getting a little inspiration for a few short years. Jesus is alive, and He has given us eternal life. Now what?

PRIEST

//HEBREWS 7:23–8:2 AND MATTHEW 12:15-21

HEBREWS 7:23–8:2

Earlier there were a lot of priests, for they died and had to be replaced. But Jesus' priesthood is permanent. He's there from now to eternity to save everyone who comes to God through him, always on the job to speak up for them.

So now we have a high priest who perfectly fits our needs: completely holy, uncompromised by sin, with authority extending as high as God's presence in heaven itself. Unlike the other high priests, he doesn't have to offer sacrifices for his own sins every day before he can get around to us and our sins. He's done it, once and for all: offered up *himself* as the sacrifice. The law appoints as high priests men who are never able to get the job done right. But this intervening command of God, which came later, appoints the Son, who is absolutely, eternally perfect.

In essence, we have just such a high priest: authoritative right alongside God, conducting worship in the one true sanctuary built by God.

MATTHEW 12:15-21

Jesus, knowing they were out to get him, moved on. A lot of people followed him, and he healed them all. He also cautioned them to keep it quiet, following guidelines set down by Isaiah:

Look well at my handpicked
     servant;
   I love him so much, take
        such delight in him.
I've placed my Spirit on him;
   he'll decree justice to the
        nations.

BIBLE READING

But he won't yell, won't raise
his voice;
    there'll be no commotion in
        the streets.
He won't walk over anyone's
    feelings,
    won't push you into a
        corner.
Before you know it, his justice
    will triumph;
    the mere sound of his name
        will signal hope, even
            among far-off
                unbelievers.

//REFLECT

In the Old Testament, the priests went before God on behalf of the people. That's what Jesus does for us. He offered the perfect sacrifice of Himself to take away our sin forever. Now He stands before the Father, pleading our case and opening the way for us to draw near to God. You may not be familiar with this characteristic of Jesus, but you count on it every time you pray. As our great High Priest, Jesus is gentle. He doesn't walk over people's feelings or push us into corners. He is the One we can count on when everyone else lets us down.

PRIEST

//MY FOCUS: HEBREWS 4:14-16

Now that we know what we have—Jesus, this great High Priest with ready access to God—let's not let it slip through our fingers. We don't have a priest who is out of touch with our reality. He's been through weakness and testing, experienced it all—all but the sin. So let's walk right up to him and get what he is so ready to give. Take the mercy, accept the help.

MY JOURNEY

//MY GOD

Sometimes I feel as if God doesn't understand me. He doesn't understand the things I go through, the feelings I have, and everything I struggle with. I have faced this many times in my life. These thoughts go through my head especially when I have experienced loss and tragedy in my family. I think, *God has no idea what this is like.*

But the truth is that God does know. First of all, He knows our deepest thoughts. We don't even need to tell Him. Secondly, we

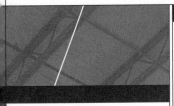

//MY PRAYER

I pray that I would come to realize the full power of God. Jesus experienced pain and heartache just as I do. He knows what I am going through and because of this, I pray that I would not wait to bring all my burdens to Him. Let me be quick to find counsel in the One who will never let me down.

have to remember that Jesus went through pain and suffering Himself as a Man here on earth. He experienced weakness and was even tested by Satan himself. God understands. Regardless of what we think or whether or not we feel like He can do anything, we need to bring our cares, our concerns, and our weaknesses before Him. As it says in Hebrews, "Take the mercy, accept the help." God's hand is reaching out, waiting for you to take hold.

//MY THOUGHTS

- In whom do I seek counsel and find comfort?
- What do I need to bring to God?

Jennifer Heath
Age: 20
Major: nursing

PRIEST

//HEBREWS 10:11-13,18-22

Every priest goes to work at the altar each day, offers the same old sacrifices year in, year out, and never makes a dent in the sin problem. As a priest, Christ made a single sacrifice for sins, and that was it! Then he sat down right beside God and waited for his enemies to cave in. . . .

Once sins are taken care of for good, there's no longer any need to offer sacrifices for them.

So, friends, we can now — without hesitation — walk right up to God, into "the Holy Place." Jesus has cleared the way by the blood of his sacrifice, acting as our priest before God. The "curtain" into God's presence is his body.

So let's do it — full of belief, confident that we're presentable inside and out.

//REFLECT

I think most Christians today are just like the priests in this passage. We go before the throne of God out of religiosity and never talk to God about what is really on our hearts or the sins we have committed. I think we figure Christ already paid for our sin, so why bring it up again? Jesus cleared the way for us to boldly approach God, yet we keep the

PRAYER & SOLITUDE

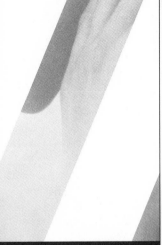

Go to the quietest place you can find and sit long enough for your heart to find peace. Enter God's Holy Place that Jesus opened up for you. As you do, meditate on the verses you just read. Think about what it means to be able to go into God's presence with confidence. The experience can be quite humbling and may draw you closer to God than you ever imagined you could be.

//THINK

curtain between our hearts and God closed. What was the point of Jesus' sacrifice if we aren't going to tell God what is on our hearts? Sure, He already knows what we are going to say, but why should we miss out on the opportunity of spending time with Someone who simply wants to hear the sound of our voice?

- What is it that makes you feel distant from God?
- What is it you are holding on to that you feel you cannot hand over to God?

Jennifer McMahon
Age: 21
Major: nursing

PRIEST

//1 JOHN 2:1-2

I write this, dear children, to guide you out of sin. But if anyone does sin, we have a Priest-Friend in the presence of the Father: Jesus Christ, righteous Jesus. When he served as a sacrifice for our sins, he solved the sin problem for good—not only ours, but the whole world's.

PRAISE & CELEBRATION

//REFLECT

Imagine for a moment that you are Jewish and living about 2,200 years ago. Your family is really big in the sheep business. You and your younger brother have the thrilling job of watching all the sheep. It's one of those days when nothing is going right. The littlest sheep keeps running off. Your younger brother keeps complaining about how much his feet hurt. When you tried to catch one of the most mischievous sheep known to man, your staff broke. On top of that, it is starting to rain. What can you do? You don't dare utter the name of the Lord; that is the job of the priest. You don't feel like you can complain, because you need these sheep not only to make a living but also to sacrifice to God for your sins. Just as these thoughts are crossing your mind, your brother runs past you and accidentally knocks you over. You become so frustrated that you turn around and hit him with all your might with your newly broken staff. You feel better, much better actually, until you see the bump on his forehead and hear him tell you he hates you. Now all you can think about is how much trouble you are going to be in when you get home and how this is just another sin you'll have to tell the priest on the day of atonement so that God won't hold it against you.

//PRAISE

Now bring yourself back to the present day. You don't have to sacrifice sheep to get right with God. Nor do you have to wait for a day of atonement to receive forgiveness for your sins. Through Jesus, our High Priest, God is available to you at all times. Today, take advantage of your access to God and worship Him throughout the day. Jesus didn't come to this earth for nothing. He came to clear the way to God. In every free moment today, go to Him and praise Him for letting you enter His presence. He is the Creator of everything. You have probably heard that before, but actually think about it: You have access to the Creator of the heavens and the earth because of Jesus. Honor Him with the praise He deserves.

Bethany Miller
Age: 19
Major: nursing

PRIEST

ACTION

//1 PETER 2:9-10

But you are the ones chosen God, chosen for the high calling of priestly work, chosen to be a holy people, God's instruments to do his work and speak out for him, to tell others of the night-and-day difference he made for you—from nothing to something, from rejected to accepted.

...CT

...belong to God, He wants ...se you. Too often we think ...means going out to the ...corners of the earth to help ...ngers. While God loves any ...of service, sometimes you ...n be most helpful to those ...losest to you. I come from a family who does not share in the love of Christ. I am also the only Christian in my closest group of friends. This makes life so hard. No one keeps me accountable, and I feel like there is nobody to share in my joy. I dream about a life where I can talk to my parents about God, where I have friends who will grow with me in Christ's love, and where I am not alone in worshiping Him. But God knew what He was doing when He put ...e in this place. He put a passion ...Jesus in me that I might ...nsform the lives of those I love.

//ACT

Before you go searching the far corners of the earth for someone to share Christ's love with, take a look at your life. Think about people you interact with every day. Do they have a passion for Christ? God needs you to help those around you. Your family and friends should be the first on your mind when it comes to putting Christ's love into action. Seek out and act on any opportunities to show how Jesus has changed your life.

As you act, be strong and not afraid. And remember, priests didn't just tell people about God. They showed others who God was through their own lives. This is your calling. God commanded us to show others the night-and-day difference He makes in our lives. So go and make the character of Jesus come alive through you to your family and friends. Show them how He is involved in your life. Changing someone's life is the most difficult thing in the world. Don't get discouraged. Remember, anything worthwhile takes time.

Tonya Corning
Age: 19
Major: nursing

PRIEST

//GENESIS 22:1-2,6-8

After all this, God tested Abraham. God said, "Abraham!"

"Yes?" answered Abraham. "I'm listening."

He said, "Take your dear son Isaac whom you love and go to the land of Moriah. Sacrifice him there as a burnt offering on one of the mountains that I'll point out to you." . . .

Abraham took the wood for the burnt offering and gave it to Isaac his son to carry. He carried the flint and the knife. The two of them went off together.

Isaac said to Abraham his father, "Father?"

"Yes, my son."

"We have flint and wood, but where's the sheep for the burnt offering?"

Abraham said, "Son, God will see to it that there's a sheep for the burnt offering." And they kept on walking together.

//REFLECT

I wonder what went through Abraham's mind as he finished putting the last piece of wood on the altar and looked at his beautiful boy, Isaac. God had blessed Abraham with his son, and now He wanted him back as a sacrifice. Was Abraham confused or angry? I wonder how he was able to build the altar and lay his son on it. But he did. When God saw Abraham's faithfulness, He stopped him before Isaac could be harmed. Abraham didn't have to sacrifice his son, but God did.

FASTING

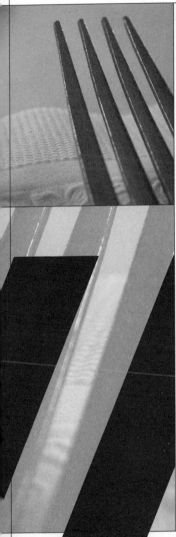

//FAST

Just as Abraham was willing to give up to God the one thing he absolutely loved, we should do the same. Today, choose something you deeply value and give it to God. Remove this one thing from your life for the rest of the day. Fast from it as an act of sacrifice. It can be your music, television, food, time, a relationship, or anything else that is very important to you. All good things are a gift from God, but unfortunately they are often the center of our worship. God wants to be the utter devotion of your entire heart, mind, body, and soul. So today, display your faith to God by offering Him one of your valued things. Fast from it for twenty-four hours and be reminded of the sacrifice Jesus offered for you on the cross.

Rebecca Rock
Age: 21
Major: nursing

//JOURNALING: HEBREWS 6:17-20

When God wanted to guarantee his promises, he gave his word, a rock-solid guarantee—God *can't* break his word. And because his word cannot change, the promise is likewise unchangeable.

We who have run for our very lives to God have every reason to grab the promised hope with both hands and never let go. It's an unbreakable spiritual lifeline, reaching past all appearances right to the very presence of God where Jesus, running on ahead of us, has taken up his permanent post as high priest for us, in the order of Melchizedek.

Jesus stands before His Father and talks to Him about us. This isn't just some religious idea. God guarantees this promise. What do you need Jesus to talk to His Father about on your behalf?

PROPHET

// HEBREWS 1:1-4 AND DEUTERONOMY 18:15-18

HEBREWS 1:1-4

Going through a long line of prophets, God has been addressing our ancestors in different ways for centuries. Recently he spoke to us directly through his Son. By his Son, God created the world in the beginning, and it will all belong to the Son at the end. This Son perfectly mirrors God, and is stamped with God's nature. He holds everything together by what he says — powerful words!

After he finished the sacrifice for sins, the Son took his honored place high in the heavens right alongside God, far higher than any angel in rank and rule.

DEUTERONOMY 18:15-18

GOD, your God, is going to raise up a prophet for you. GOD will raise him up from among your kinsmen, a prophet like me. Listen obediently to him. This is what you asked GOD, your God, for at Horeb on the day you were all gathered at the mountain and said, "We can't hear any more from GOD, our God; we can't stand seeing any more fire. We'll die!"

And GOD said to me, "They're right; they've spoken the truth. I'll raise up for them a prophet like you from their kinsmen. I'll tell him what to say and he will pass on to them everything I command him."

BIBLE READING

//REFLECT

In the Old Testament, God established three positions of authority to guide His people: priests, kings, and prophets. The priests led the people into God's presence through sacrifices. Kings led the people as God's ruling authority. And the prophets were God's mouthpieces. They spoke for God to the people. When Jesus came to earth, He filled all three offices once and for all. This week we will explore Jesus as God's final word to the human race. He is not just a prophet; He is the last and greatest of the prophets, for who can speak for God better than God in human flesh? As God's final word, how does Jesus speak to the world today?

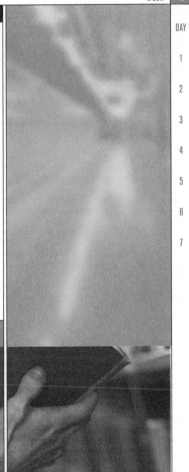

PROPHET

//ACTS 3:19-23

Now it's time to change your ways! Turn to face God so he can wipe away your sins, pour out showers of blessing to refresh you, and send you the Messiah he prepared for you, namely, Jesus. For the time being he must remain out of sight in heaven until everything is restored to order again just the way God, through the preaching of his holy prophets of old, said it would be. Moses, for instance, said, "Your God will raise up for you a prophet just like me from your family. Listen to every word he speaks to you. Every last living soul who refuses to listen to that prophet will be wiped out from the people."

//REFLECT

I've had a couple of opportunities to go backpacking in the High Sierras in California. During these trips, I learned how to listen to God. When I came down from the mountains and started college in the Los Angeles area, I found that it took much more effort to hear God's voice. I get so busy that my prayer life can turn into a one-way conversation in which I do all the talking and never take time to listen. Yet real discipleship begins with listening to Jesus. If I'm serious about following Him, I have to slow myself down enough to hear Him.

PRAYER & SOLITUDE

//PRAY

Make your time of prayer a real conversation. Don't do all the talking. Listen for the voice of Jesus, God's great Prophet. Ask God to take away the things that distract you from simply sitting at His feet and listening. When Jesus was alive, people didn't always like what He had to say. When we listen for His voice, He may say things that make us uncomfortable. That's when we have to take the next step and obey. According to Moses, the way we respond to Jesus, God's Prophet, will determine our destiny. How will we react to what He says?

Audra Jordan
Age: 22
Major: biblical studies

PROPHET

ACTION

// 2 CORINTHIANS 5:19-21

God put the world square with himself through the Messiah, giving the world a fresh start by offering forgiveness of sins. God has given us the task of telling everyone what he is doing. We're Christ's representatives. God uses us to persuade men and women to drop their differences and enter into God's work of making things right between them. We're speaking for Christ himself now: Become friends with God; he's already a friend with you.

How? you say. In Christ. God put the wrong on him who never did anything wrong, so we could be put right with God.

//REFLECT

- What does it mean to receive a fresh start? How did your life change when you entered into a relationship with Christ?
- Think about your friends. Do they know that you are a Christian? How will they come to know about Christ if you don't take a risk and share Him with them?

//ACT

Being God's representative is a great honor, but with that honor comes responsibility. If you don't act as Christ's voice to your friends, who will? Think of one friend who does not have a relationship with Christ and go share your story with him. Tell him about what Christ has done and is doing in your life. The most important thing is to be honest. You are not trying to trick anyone. Don't get stressed out. God calls His followers to do this. Not only that, but He will give you the right words to say. Be Christ's voice today and help your friend get off to a fresh start and new life in Christ!

Evan Sheldon
Age: 21
Major: biblical studies

PROPHET

Later on that day, the disciples had gathered together, but, fearful of the Jews, had locked all the doors in the house. Jesus entered, stood among them, and said, "Peace to you." Then he showed them his hands and side.

The disciples, seeing the Master with their own eyes, were exuberant. Jesus repeated his greeting: "Peace to you. Just as the Father sent me, I send you."

// REFLECT

Jesus' message was more words. He embodied His Fa character. Both His words actions revealed God to us. I Jesus sends you and me, jus His Father sent Him. This me we must embody Jesus' charact so that others will come to know God through our witness.

One thing prevents us from answering Jesus' call: fear. We're afraid of how people will respond. But Jesus gently takes away our fear and replaces it with His peace. In Him we now have a joy that cannot be held back. And this is what we share with others.

FASTING

//THE NEXT LEVEL

- What truths about God did you discover during your fast?
- What did you discover about yourself?
- What did you hear God telling you to do as a result of the time you spent fasting from fear?

Leah Carlitz
Age: 19
Majors: youth ministry; biblical studies

//FAST

...ay, take a fast from fear so you ...be enabled to actively express ...Jesus is in your life. Pay close ...ntion to your thoughts and ...tions throughout the day. Fear ... be subtle. Ask God to make ...sensitive to it and to give you ...conquering peace and courage ...overcome it.

As you fast from fear, find some Bible verses that will encourage you to trust in God and find your peace and joy in Him. Every time you feel fear welling up inside, go back to the verses you found. Listen to the truth of God's Word rather than your fear. Throughout the day, focus your mind on the call to embody Jesus' character. Express your joy through conversations and actions.

PROPHET

//MY FOCUS: HEBREWS 2:1-4

It's crucial that we keep a firm grip on what we've heard so that we don't drift off. If the old message delivered by the angels was valid and nobody got away with anything, do you think we can risk neglecting this latest message, this magnificent salvation? First of all, it was delivered in person by the Master, then accurately passed on to us by those who heard it from him. All the while God was validating it with gifts through the Holy Spirit, all sorts of signs and miracles, as he saw fit.

MY JOURNEY

//MY GOD

What if I've already drifted off? I believe in Jesus, and I try to do my best to follow Him, but I am so easily distracted. The busyness of life pulls me in every direction except the one I need to be pulled in—toward Him. And it's so easy to blame the world. I get this "poor pitiful me" syndrome where nothing is my fault. There's always some reason that I had to lie to my friend or take just one more glance at that girl.

Then I am reminded of the message of Jesus. All of a sudden, my petty complaints and excuses fade into the background. Who am I to stand and explain to God that I failed to share the gospel because I didn't get enough sleep the night before? How could I be so blind as to think that my headache excused me from the mission to proclaim Jesus?

//MY PRAYER

Father, forgive me for being so preoccupied with the cares of the world. I want to be much more disciplined and much less distracted. Thank You for always staying faithful, even when I am not. Teach me to rise above my weaknesses and live out of Your strength. Remind me that I am only the clay and You are the potter. Thank You for the gift of Your Son, and please help me proclaim Him to those I come in contact with.

Adam Frazier
Age: 20
Major: biblical studies

The truth is, this message stretches far beyond any of our shortcomings. It is proclaimed by God's power, not ours. In our weakness, He is strong. In our failures, He succeeds. May I be the kind of person who proclaims the good news even in my weakest moments, relying on His strength. Forsaking my own agendas, I will join with those who have gone before me in testifying to this wondrous message of redemption.

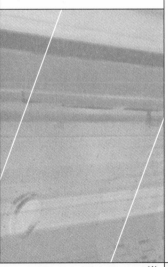

PROPHET

We got the basics from
    Moses,
  and then this exuberant
    giving and receiving,
This endless knowing and
    understanding—
  all this came through Jesus,
    the Messiah.
No one has ever seen God,
  not so much as a glimpse.
This one-of-a-kind God-
    Expression,
  who exists at the very heart
    of the Father,
  has made him plain as day.

PRAISE &
CELEBRATION

//REFLECT

Prophets spoke for God and revealed Him to the people. Jesus didn't just tell us about God. He showed us the Father through His words and deeds. He made Him plain as day to us. That's why He was God's final word. But of course, you know this by now. The real question is this: How will we respond to this Prophet?

//PRAISE

Today's exercise will take more than seven minutes. Open your Bible to one of the four Gospels: Matthew, Mark, Luke, or John. Find a part in one of the Gospels where Jesus does a lot of talking. (This will be easy if you have a red-letter Bible, where red ink highlights Jesus' words.) If you don't know where to look, try Luke 12–18. Now start reading. But don't just read the words; interact with them. Watch for the ways Jesus reveals His Father. Listen to how His words describe God's passion and priorities. As you see the Father through the Son, worship Him. Thank Him and praise Him and do whatever it takes to show your love and adoration for Him. Do this for as long as your schedule will let you. Responding to Jesus' words means more than letting Him clean up your life. Listening to Him should leave you on your face, worshiping His holy name.

//JOURNALING: JOHN 17:24-26

"Father, I want those you
        gave me
To be with me, right where
        I am,
So they can see my glory, the
        splendor you gave me,
Having loved me
Long before there ever was a
        world.
Righteous Father, the world
        has never known you,
But I have known you, and
        these disciples know
That you sent me on this
        mission.
I have made your very being
        known to them—
Who you are and what you
        do—
And continue to make it
        known,
So that your love for me
Might be in them
Exactly as I am in them."

God is still speaking today
through His greatest Prophet,
Jesus. How will you react to what
He says? How can you also be
God's voice to the world?

CONTRIBUTORS

Mark Tabb, general editor

Devotions: those not written by students

Author of nine books, including *Greater Than: Unconventional Thoughts on the Infinite God*

Favorite book: *Loving God* by Charles Colson

How I will make a difference in the world: by writing books that force people to think

STUDENT CONTRIBUTORS, AZUSA PACIFIC UNIVERSITY:

Katrina Anker

Devotion: Praise & Celebration—God in Flesh, pages 14–15

Age: 20

Major: nursing

Favorite book: *The Return of the Prodigal Son* by Henri Nouwen

How I will make a difference in the world: by trying to demonstrate God's compassion and love every day, especially through nursing

Courtney Bacon

Devotion: Fasting—Obedient, pages 68–69

Age: 21

Major: Christian ministries

Favorite book: *Rascal* by Sterling North

How I will make a difference in the world: I plan to make a difference in the world through my hospitality, generosity, and grace.

Christopher Bunting
  Devotion: Action—Alive, pages 108–109
  Age: 19
  Major: communications
  Favorite book: *Into the Wild* by Jon Krakauer
  How I will make a difference in the world: by letting people know
    that I appreciate them

Leah Carlitz
  Devotion: Fasting—Prophet, pages 138–139
  Age: 19
  Majors: youth ministry; biblical studies
  Favorite book: *Hinds' Feet on High Places* by Hannah Hurnard
  How I will make a difference in the world: by learning how to show
    others what it means to be real with one another and experience
    fellowship the way God designed it

Christopher Cazares
  Devotion: My Journey—Sacrifice, pages 100–101
  Age: 21
  Majors: English; philosophy
  Favorite book: *Crime and Punishment* by Fyodor Dostoevsky
  How I will make a difference in the world: I will work toward
    reversing the stereotype of Christians as being ignorant so that
    we are taken seriously and put in a position in which we can
    better address the needs of our society.

Joy Collins
  Devotion: Praise & Celebration—Sacrifice, pages 94–95
  Age: 20
  Major: cinema broadcast arts
  Favorite book: *I Know Why the Caged Bird Sings* by Maya Angelou
  How I will make a difference in the world: by doing everything
    possible to help those around me

Janelle Comfort

> Devotion: Praise & Celebration—Obedient, pages 72–73
>
> Age: 20
>
> Major: youth ministry
>
> Favorite book: *Blue Like Jazz* by Donald Miller
>
> How I will make a difference in the world: by encouraging and empowering young women to find their value in Christ and through that value to live a revolutionary life

Tonya Corning

> Devotion: Action—Priest, pages 126–127
>
> Age: 19
>
> Major: nursing
>
> Favorite book: *The Canterbury Tales* by Geoffrey Chaucer
>
> How I will make a difference in the world: by unconditionally loving and caring for everyone

Tamra Danenhauer

> Devotion: Prayer & Solitude—Sacrifice, pages 92–93
>
> Age: 21
>
> Major: communications
>
> Favorite book: *Anna Karenina* by Leo Tolstoy
>
> How I will make a difference in the world: I will make a difference by always striving to glorify God and following the prompting of His Spirit in my life.

Sarah Day

> Devotion: Prayer & Solitude—Holy, pages 82–83
>
> Age: 21
>
> Major: natural science
>
> Favorite book: *Pride and Prejudice* by Jane Austen
>
> How I will make a difference in the world: by enlightening students to the wonder of God's creation through science

Kyle Dunning
> Devotion: Fasting—Unpredictable, pages 52–53
> Age: 18
> Major: psychology
> Favorite book: *Celebration of Discipline* by Richard Foster
> How I will make a difference in the world: by worshiping God

Joseph A. Ellis IV
> Devotion: My Journey—Unpredictable, pages 58–59
> Age: 21
> Major: psychology
> Favorite book: *And Then There Were None* by Agatha Christie
> How I will make a difference in the world: I plan to go into counseling, and I hope to be able to help others and make a difference in their lives.

Susanna R. Eskridge
> Devotion: My Journey—Servant King, pages 22–23
> Age: 19
> Major: communications
> Favorite book: *The Unbearable Lightness of Being* by Milan Kundera
> How I will make a difference in the world: by giving, not taking, and by living my life reflecting Christ's love in all I say and do

Adam Frazier
> Devotion: My Journey—Prophet, pages 140–141
> Age: 20
> Major: biblical studies
> Favorite book: *Godric* by Frederick Buechner
> How I will make a difference in the world: by questioning everything

John Gaquin
> Devotion: Action—Countercultural, pages 38–39
> Age: 23
> Major: communications
> Favorite book: *The Grapes of Wrath* by John Steinbeck
> How I will make a difference in the world: by being the best friend that I can be

Yvania A. Garcia
> Devotion: My Journey—Alive, pages 114–115
> Age: 20
> Majors: journalism; political science
> Favorite book: *The Catcher in the Rye* by J. D. Salinger
> How I will make a difference in the world: by loving all those around me and accepting them for who they are

Jennifer Heath
> Devotion: My Journey—Priest, pages 120–121
> Age: 20
> Major: nursing
> Favorite book: *The Journey of Desire* by John Eldredge
> How I will make a difference in the world: by making Christ known through every moment of my life and spreading His love to each and every person I come in contact with

Audra Jordan
> Devotion: Prayer & Solitude—Prophet, pages 134–135
> Age: 22
> Major: biblical studies
> Favorite book: *The Giving Tree* by Shel Silverstein
> How I will make a difference in the world: by carrying God's love with compassion, commitment, and courage

Hannah Kelmis

    Devotion: Prayer & Solitude—Countercultural, pages 40–41

    Age: 22

    Major: English

    Favorite book: *Till We Have Faces* by C. S. Lewis

    How I will make a difference in the world: by proving that God
        cares about people, not just their salvation, and doing my part
        to break down the barriers between the church and the world
        through real relationships instead of programs and tracts

Ilise Lauman

    Devotion: Action—Sacrifice, pages 96–97

    Age: 19

    Major: communications

    Favorite book: *God's Smuggler* by Brother Andrew

    How I will make a difference in the world: I strive to make my
        conduct and responses toward people merciful and sensitive.

Garrett Lowe

    Devotion: Action—Unpredictable, pages 56–57

    Age: 20

    Majors: business; premed

    Favorite books: Tom Clancy novels

    How I will make a difference in the world: I will make a difference
        by not judging people by their actions but by their sincerity.
        There is no need to point fingers when we also live in a pool of
        sin. Everyone is God's creation.

Dennis Marinello

    Devotion: Prayer & Solitude—Unpredictable, pages 54–55

    Age: 19

    Major: undeclared

    Favorite book: the Bible

    How I will make a difference in the world: I will live to glorify the
        Lord and will introduce people to Jesus.

Jennifer McMahon

Devotion: Prayer & Solitude—Priest, pages 122–123

Age: 21

Major: nursing

Favorite book: *The Scarlet Pimpernel* by Baroness Orczy

How I will make a difference in the world: by loving people as they are and having meaningful relationships with them

Jessica Meydag

Devotion: Action—God in Flesh, pages 12–13

Age: 23

Major: nursing

Favorite book: *The Count of Monte Cristo* by Alexandre Dumas

How I will make a difference in the world: by bringing peace and hope to those who are going through pain and illness

Bethany Miller

Devotion: Praise & Celebration—Priest, pages 124–125

Age: 19

Major: nursing

Favorite book: *Anna Karenina* by Leo Tolstoy

How I will make a difference in the world: by working as a nurse and being able to comfort and care for people in their most vulnerable moments

Annie Moddelmog

Devotion: Prayer & Solitude—God in Flesh, pages 8–9

Age: 21

Major: nursing

Favorite book: *Praying God's Word* by Beth Moore

How I will make a difference in the world: by loving those who need love the most

Crissa Nelson
    Devotion: Praise & Celebration—Servant King, pages 30–31
    Age: 18
    Major: journalism
    Favorite book: the Bible; Favorite novel: *Divine Secrets of the Ya-Ya
        Sisterhood* by Rebecca Wells
    How I will make a difference in the world: one prayer at a time

Emily Penner
    Devotion: Fasting—God in Flesh, pages 10–11
    Age: 20
    Major: nursing
    Favorite book: *Redeeming Love* by Francine Rivers
    How I will make a difference in the world: I want to invest in,
        empower, and love people by sharing God's love and by
        providing health care to people who cannot get any.

Rachel Pietka
    Devotion: Action—Holy, pages 78–79
    Age: 21
    Major: English with a concentration in literature
    Favorite book: *Les Misérables* by Victor Hugo
    How I will make a difference in the world: I want to make
        a difference by serving others, particularly the poor and
        underprivileged, through education.

Andrew Porter
    Devotion: Action—Obedient, pages 64–65
    Age: 21
    Major: youth ministry
    Favorite book: *The Giving Tree* by Shel Silverstein
    How I will make a difference in the world: by loving

Nadia Ramirez

> Devotion: Fasting—Holy, pages 80–81
>
> Age: 23
>
> Major: international business
>
> Favorite book: *What's So Amazing About Grace?* by Philip Yancey
>
> How I will make a difference in the world: I believe that we have the opportunity to change this world by our daily activities. Making a difference in these times all boils down to the golden rule: Treat others as you would like them to treat you. Being considerate and thoughtful of others is how I plan to make a difference in this self-involved culture.

Dustin Reynolds

> Devotion: My Journey—Holy, pages 86–87
>
> Age: 20
>
> Major: biblical studies
>
> Favorite book: *Tuesdays with Morrie* by Mitch Albom
>
> How I will make a difference in the world: by trying to continuously see people as Christ did

Amy Rice

> Devotion: My Journey—God in Flesh, pages 16–17
>
> Age: 21
>
> Major: nursing
>
> Favorite book: *Why Not Women?* by Loren Cunningham and David Joel Hamilton
>
> How I will make a difference in the world: by following whatever God's plan is for me to make a difference for His kingdom

Lindsey Rinehart

Devotion: Praise & Celebration—Unpredictable, pages 50–51

Age: 19

Major: undeclared (focused toward nutrition or athletic training)

Favorite book: the book of Psalms in the Bible

How I will make a difference in the world: I want to resemble Christ's love. Not to sound cliché, but I want people to look at me and know that there is something different. I want them to ask what's different, and I want to be able to tell them how Christ has impacted my life.

Rebecca Rock

Devotion: Fasting—Priest, pages 128–129

Age: 21

Major: nursing

Favorite book: *Redeeming Love* by Francine Rivers

How I will make a difference in the world: by sharing Christ's love with those who are suffering

Henry Romero

Devotion: My Journey—Countercultural, pages 44–45

Age: 21

Major: English

Favorite book: *The Great Gatsby* by F. Scott Fitzgerald

How I will make a difference in the world: by exemplifying Christ in all that I do

Carissa Sechrist

Devotion: Prayer & Solitude—Servant King, pages 26–27

Age: 21

Major: communications

Favorite books: anything by Cerella D. Sechrist

How I will make a difference in the world: The biggest difference a person can make in the world, and in themselves, is to live each day as a choice—to choose joy, to choose to live out loud, and to choose life.

Evan Sheldon
   Devotion: Action—Prophet, pages 136–137
   Age: 21
   Major: biblical studies
   Favorite book: *Perelandra* by C. S. Lewis
   How I will make a difference in the world: by critically evaluating
      and questioning everything that comes across my path

Peter Sherman
   Devotion: Prayer & Solitude—Obedient, pages 66–67
   Age: 21
   Major: youth ministry
   Favorite book: *A Prayer for Owen Meany* by John Irving
   How I will make a difference in the world: by allowing God's love
      to shine out through me

Nicholas Thorn-Sermeno
   Devotion: Fasting—Obedient, pages 68–69
   Age: 22
   Major: biblical studies
   Favorite book: *The Count of Monte Cristo* by Alexandre Dumas
   How I will make a difference in the world: by loving people the
      way God has loved me

Jessica van der Stad
   Devotion: Fasting—Servant King, pages 24–25
   Age: 19
   Major: communications with an emphasis in journalism
   Favorite book: *The Giver* by Lois Lowry
   How I will make a difference in the world: by living in the moment,
      refusing to have regrets, and loving like there is no tomorrow

Shannon Van Vorst
  Devotion: Fasting—Alive, pages 110–111
  Age: 19
  Major: communications
  Favorite book: *Redeeming Love* by Francine Rivers
  How I will make a difference in the world: by loving others
    unconditionally

Renee Vaupel
  Devotion: Fasting—Sacrifice, pages 98–99
  Age: 20
  Major: communications
  Favorite books: the LEFT BEHIND series by Jerry B. Jenkins and Tim
    LaHaye
  How I will make a difference in the world: by being honest with
    myself and with others so that they may see the truth about
    God's gracious love

Christina Vickers
  Devotion: Prayer & Solitude—Alive, pages 106–107
  Age: 20
  Major: communications
  Favorite book: *Their Eyes Were Watching God* by Zora Neale Hurston
  How I will make a difference in the world: by showing people that
    they have more value and are more loved than they can even
    imagine

Liz Wade
  Devotion: My Journey—Obedient, pages 70–71
  Age: 21
  Major: youth ministry
  Favorite book: *The Grapes of Wrath* by John Steinbeck
  How I will make a difference in the world: I want to make a
    difference by living with constant joy from the Lord! I plan
    to teach high school classes regarding the Bible and life
    application and participate in missions in Ethiopia.

Jenna Willems
Devotion: Action—Servant King, pages 28–29
Age: 20
Major: communications with an emphasis in interpersonal/
organizational; cognate in marketing/business
Favorite book: *The Notebook* by Nicholas Sparks
How I will make a difference in the world: by being a positive
influence on younger children